Recipes from a New England Inn

Recipes from a New England Inn

by Trudy Cutrone

Illustrated by Margaret Parker

Recipes from a New England Inn

Published by Country Roads Press
P.O. Box 286, Lower Main Street
Castine, Maine 04421

Designed by Janet Mecca.
Library of Congress Catalog Card No. 92-071641
ISBN 1-56626-012-4

Printed in the United States of America.
10 9 8 7 6 5 4 3

To Frank and Peter with love and thanks

Table of Contents

Preface

*N*othing quite piques the appetite like a walk or a drive in the country. And nothing quite satisfies hunger like a meal at a country inn. This truth was brought home to me the first time I dined at the Snowvillage Inn. I sat in a cozy, chalet-style dining room, feasting on French silk pie, watching the sun set over the White Mountains. I knew I would have to make the Snowvillage Inn an integral part of my life.

Today, the Snowvillage Inn is the home of my cooking school. Three times a year, my students and I descend on the kitchen. Trudy welcomes us with the graciousness and hospitality that are the hallmark of her inn. From the first chocolate chip cookie (Trudy places a cookie basket in the rooms of arriving guests) to the last buttery bite of apple strudel, I know that during my stay I will dine like a king.

In this day and age of designer food and celebrity chefs, Trudy's style of cooking – good home cooking – has almost become an endangered species. Her food is rooted in the cuisine of her native Austria. But her love of fresh fruits and vegetables harmonizes with the health-consciousness of modern Americans. All of Trudy's breads and desserts are baked on the premises. The inn's garden supplies her with edible flowers and fresh herbs. Trudy's food is simple but never simple-minded, elegant without being stuffy. It's the kind of lovingly prepared, home-cooked food most of us wish we'd grown up on.

And now I have discovered Trudy is a talented writer as well. It gives me great pleasure to introduce her new cookbook. I look forward to making her Jaeger Rouladen (spicy beef rolls) and Nuernburger Lebkuchen (spicy honey cookies). Best of all, I won't have to wait until my next trip to the White Mountains to enjoy Trudy's fabulous chocolate chip cookies!

— *Steve Raichlen*

Introduction

Snowvillage Inn, located five miles south of Conway, New Hampshire, offers a magnificent view of the White Mountains. It is an ideal romantic getaway place. There is no traffic, no noise, just birds, crickets, and the wind playing in the pines.

Because the inn started out as a writer's retreat back in 1916, books and cozy places to read abound, and each of the eighteen guestrooms is named after an author. Come and see the Robert Frost room with its twelve windows looking straight out at Mount Washington. What a place for a honeymoon!

When we bought the inn in 1986, we felt the need to do something wildly different. We gladly left good careers behind (Frank was a corporate executive, Peter a petroleum engineer, and Trudy a German teacher) to pool our talents, work hard as a team, and at the same time enjoy this beautiful area.

Running an inn is a labor of love. We each had to quickly find our natural niche: Peter, the maintenance, outdoor work, and computer; Frank, the office and playing Ta-Ka Radi with the guests; and Trudy, the kitchen. There was much to learn and the work was hard, but eventually everything improved. Guests began to say the inn was special. They loved the view, the excellent service, and Boris and Natasha, the big white inn dogs. They loved the friendliness of the innkeepers and the staff. They loved the whole atmosphere of the inn and the feeling of warmth the minute they came in the door.

And they loved the food. Many guests asked for and received recipes. Many suggested that Trudy write a cookbook. As the message spread, we experienced the joy of seeing Snowvillage written up in *Bon Appetit, Gourmet, Yankee Travel Guide, Skiing,* the *Boston Globe, Country Living,* the *Los Angeles Times,* and the *New York Post.* We received recognition as a finalist in the Uncle Ben's competition. And as this book goes to press, articles are appearing in *Yankee Magazine* and *The Washingtonian.*

In response to all that encouragement and all those requests, Peter and Frank conspired to give Trudy the time to put her labor of love in writing. This collection of the best recipes from the Snowvillage Inn kitchen is the happy result. We hope you enjoy it!

— Frank, Trudy, and Peter Cutrone
Snowvillage Inn
Snowville, New Hampshire 03849
800-447-4345

Hors d'Oeuvres

When you cook, you are not just working on food,
you are working on yourself,
you are working on others.

Shunryu Suzuki-roshi

Kate's Last-Minute Artichoke Spread

1 14-ounce can artichoke hearts, water packed
1 clove garlic, peeled and mashed
3 tablespoons good mayonnaise
Hungarian paprika

Drain the artichokes and squeeze out the water from each one. Chop finely and transfer them to a small saucepan. Add the garlic and mayonnaise. Blend well.

To blend and enhance the flavors, warm over low heat, stirring constantly. Do not let it boil. Turn spread into a serving bowl, sprinkle with paprika, and offer with your favorite crackers.

A house classic, this recipe is in constant demand by our guests who try to guess the secret flavorings. There aren't any. It's fast, simple, and just plain wonderful.

Serves 10 to 12

Stuffed Mushrooms with Spinach and Cheese

12 medium mushrooms
1 strip bacon
1 teaspoon butter
½ cup onion, minced
1 clove garlic, crushed
5 ounces frozen spinach, defrosted, squeezed
   dry, and chopped
1 ounce Swiss cheese, grated
1 ounce ricotta cheese
1 tablespoon grated Parmesan cheese
2 tablespoons fresh minced parsley
Salt and pepper to taste

This is an easy and delicious variation on a perennial favorite.

Wipe and stem the mushrooms. Arrange the caps, hollow side up, in a greased baking dish.

In a small skillet, fry the bacon. Remove and drain on paper towel. Mince and set aside. Add the butter to the bacon fat and add the onion. Sauté, partially covered, for 20 minutes or until translucent. Add garlic and spinach and simmer for another few minutes. Transfer mixture to a bowl and cool slightly before adding the cheeses, parsley, and bacon bits. Mix well and adjust the taste with salt and pepper if needed.

Preheat oven to 400°. Stuff the mushroom caps with the cheese and spinach mixture and bake in the upper half of the oven for 8 to 10 minutes. Serve hot.

Serves 4

Beef Teriyaki

1 cup Tamari soy sauce
1 teaspoon fresh grated ginger
1 teaspoon crushed garlic
1 to 2 tablespoons brown sugar (enough to
   balance the salt in the soy sauce)
1 pound beef tenderloin tips, cut in small cubes
2 to 3 tablespoons sesame or vegetable oil

Mix Tamari, ginger, garlic, and brown sugar in
a bowl. Add the beef and marinate for at least 4
hours. Drain and quickly brown the beef in hot
oil. Serve hot, with toothpicks.

This treat is especially nice before a seafood dinner.

Serves 10 to 12

Mushroom Paté

1 cup (8 ounces) butter
1 cup minced onion
3 pounds mushrooms, rinsed and finely chopped
1 cup Burgundy wine
½ cup Madeira wine
3 or 4 bay leaves
1 teaspoon fresh thyme or ½ teaspoon dried
   thyme
Pinch of grated nutmeg
1 teaspoon freshly ground pepper
1½ teaspoons salt
¼ to ½ cup heavy cream

¼ cup minced red onion
1 tablespoon minced parsley

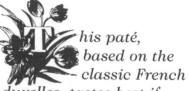

This paté, based on the classic French duxelles, tastes best if prepared the day before you plan to serve it.

The mushrooms here needn't be totally fresh. In fact, the telltale browning of older mushrooms adds to the color and flavor of the paté (and they're great for soups, too).

Melt the butter in a large skillet. Sauté the onions, covered, for about 20 minutes, then add mushrooms, wines, bay leaves, thyme, nutmeg, salt, and pepper. Cook over high heat until mushrooms have wilted, about 10 minutes. Reduce heat and simmer uncovered, stirring occasionally, for 45 minutes to 1 hour until most of the liquid has been reduced and the mixture has thickened. Cool briefly.

In batches, purée the cooked ingredients in the blender, adding a bit of the heavy cream when needed. The mixture should be as smooth and creamy as baby food. At this point, adjust the taste with more salt and pepper. The paté should be well seasoned.

Transfer the paté to a sieve lined with fine cloth (a piece of old cotton will do). Place the sieve over a pot or bowl and drain the paté overnight in the refrigerator.

Before serving, carefully twist the tips of the cloth and squeeze out as much liquid as possible (don't discard this mushroom/wine liquid; it's wonderful when added to a beef sauce). Transfer the paté to an attractive serving dish such as a ceramic quiche pan, filling it completely and flattening the top. Sprinkle with minced onion and parsley and serve with crackers.

Serves 20

Eggplant Paté

1 small eggplant
1 red pepper
1 small red onion
3 tablespoons good olive oil
Salt and pepper to taste
4 tablespoons chopped black olives
1 tablespoon minced parsley
Crackers or toasted French bread

Wrap eggplant in foil and bake at 350° for
1 hour or until soft. Cool, peel, and chop into
chunks. Place in the food processor.

Meanwhile, roast the red pepper until black.
Peel off the skin while holding the pepper in a
bowl of cold water. The roasting adds a great
flavor, but if you prefer, use the pepper raw.
Seed, chop, and add it to the eggplant. Chop the
onion and add that to the eggplant, along with
the oil and a little salt and pepper. Purée until
smooth. Taste and correct the seasoning with
more salt and pepper if needed. Chill.

Transfer paté to an attractive serving bowl, top
with black olives and parsley. Serve with your
favorite crackers or bite-size pieces of toasted
French bread.

Serves 10 to 12

*This recipe is
based on one
contributed
by Lori Matava, a guest
who loves to cook and
entertain. While she was
checking out, we excitedly
began to chat about hors
d'oeuvres, holding up
some other guests in the
process. I handed her
some recipes. "Send me
some of yours," I called
after her as she left. She
did and they are all
wonderful, but this one
is by far our favorite.*

Crudités and Dill Dip

Crudités

1 small jicama (Mexican root vegetable), peeled and cut like French fries
1 cup broccoli florets, blanched
1 cup cauliflower florets, blanched
1 red pepper, julienned
3 medium carrots, cut in sticks
3 celery stalks, peeled and cut in sticks
10 small mushrooms
10 radishes

Other choices might be green onions, green peppers, peeled and seeded cucumbers, yellow peppers, zucchini – you name it!

Dip

½ cup sour cream
½ cup good mayonnaise
2 tablespoons grated onion
2 tablespoons fresh minced dill
White ground pepper to taste

Mix the above ingredients and chill for at least 3 hours to blend flavors. Serve with a tray of your favorite vegetables, attractively arranged, alternating different colors and textures.

When I first started cooking for our inn, Tanya Blymeyer, daughter of the former owner, was my first teacher. She stuck it out with me for two weeks, showing me not only how to cook, but also how to shop, order, take inventory, plan menus, and handle all those things a kitchen manager needs to know. Most importantly, she showed me how not to lose my nerve. This Dill Dip is one of the many recipes I inherited from Tanya. We still use it routinely, and whenever we do I think of her. Thank you, Tanya!

Serves 10

Dilled Crabmeat on Cucumber Rounds

1 European cucumber
½ pound crabmeat, drained and squeezed
   very dry
1 green onion, minced
2 tablespoons fresh minced dill
Juice of ½ lemon
½ celery stalk, minced
1 plum tomato, seeded and chopped
¼ cup mayonnaise
A few drops Tabasco sauce
Salt and pepper to taste
Diced red pepper, pimento, or red caviar for
   garnish

Score the cucumber with a fork or zester
(optional). Cut into ¼-inch slices and lay flat
between two layers of paper towels to absorb
moisture.

In a small bowl, combine crabmeat, onion, dill,
lemon juice, celery, tomato, mayonnaise, Tabasco,
salt, and pepper. Mix very well, cover, and chill
for an hour to blend flavors.

Just before serving, sprinkle cucumber slices
lightly with salt and pepper. Top each slice with
1 to 1½ teaspoons crabmeat mixture, place your
favorite red garnish in center, and serve.

An attractive, light hors d'oeuvre, especially nice for the Christmas holidays because of the green and red colors.

Makes about 36 rounds

Erika's Seafood Cheese Delight

2 8-ounce packages cream cheese, softened to
  room temperature
¼ cup good mayonnaise
2 tablespoons lemon juice
1 teaspoon Worcestershire sauce
1 clove garlic, crushed
½ cup chopped celery
1 tablespoon chopped chives
1 4½-ounce can shrimp, drained
1 6-ounce can crabmeat, drained; set aside ¼
  of it
¾ cup chili sauce
2 tablespoons sweet pickle relish
2 tablespoons minced parsley

In a bowl, stir cream cheese until smooth. Add
mayonnaise, lemon juice, Worcestershire sauce,
garlic, celery, chives, shrimp, and three-quarters
of the crabmeat. Mix well. Spread into a 9-inch
round serving dish (we use an attractive quiche
plate) and chill for at least 1 hour.

Mix the chili sauce with the pickle relish and
spread evenly over the chilled seafood/cheese
mixture. Mix parsley with remaining crabmeat
and sprinkle this on top. Serve with your favorite
crackers.

Serves 20

When our
Oregonian
granddaughter
Erika was born (finally,
after an endless three-
week delay), we were so
happy and relieved we
immediately celebrated
her arrival with a
champagne party right
in the hospital. Somebody
brought this delicious
hors d'oeuvre, and that's
how it got its name.

Perrin's Shrimp Toast

6 ounces raw shrimp, shelled, deveined, and
   rinsed
1 tablespoon cornstarch
2 to 3 stems of scallions, minced
1 teaspoon sesame oil
Salt and pepper to taste
1 egg white
6 white bread slices, crust removed
2 to 3 tablespoons cooking oil

Purée shrimp in the food processor, then add
cornstarch, scallions, sesame oil, salt, and pepper.
Purée a few more seconds until well blended.
Transfer mixture to a bowl.

Beat the egg white to soft peaks and fold into
the shrimp. Spread this mixture on the bread
slices (spread it a bit higher in the center;
it will level out when cut), then cut each slice
diagonally, dividing it into four triangles.

In a heavy frying pan, heat the cooking oil, then
fry triangles, shrimp side down, for no longer
than 45 seconds. Turn, fry bread side down for
another 15 seconds.

Drain shrimp toast on paper towels and arrange
on platter. Serve hot.

Serves 6 to 8

When our son Lee and his Chinese fiancée decided to have their wedding reception at the inn, I cast around for a very special cook, for two reasons. Naturally, I wanted to be out of the kitchen on that day. Also I wanted someone who could do a Chinese meal in Jing Fang's honor. Not the corner store take-out variety, but something truly delicious and elegant. After a detour or two, I found Perrin Long, who has his own catering business in Ossipee, New Hampshire. He designed and cooked a dinner that would have done the last emperor proud. This shrimp toast was just one of the introductions. How do you say "wonderful" in Chinese?

Hot Asparagus Rolls

3 ounces blue cheese
8 ounces cream cheese, warmed to room
   temperature
1 egg
20 slices white bread
1 15-ounce can asparagus spears
½ pound butter, melted

Blend blue cheese, cream cheese, and egg until smooth (best done in a food processor). Trim crusts off bread. Flatten each slice with a rolling pin, then spread with cheese mixture. Place one asparagus spear on the bottom of each slice and roll up. Place each roll, seam side down, on an ungreased baking sheet. Partially freeze rolls, then slice each roll into thirds (the freezing prevents cheese from oozing out while slicing). Rolls can be done ahead of time to this point, frozen completely, and stored in plastic bags. They freeze beautifully.

Preheat oven to 400°. Place asparagus rolls on a greased baking sheet and brush them generously with melted butter. Bake for 15 to 20 minutes until lightly browned (20 to 25 minutes if frozen solid). Serve at once and watch them disappear — fast!

Back in Pittsburgh, when the word "gourmet" made me genuflect and my only cooking tools were the pressure cooker and the Crockpot, I had a neighbor who was a culinary sophisticate. Nobody, but nobody, could beat her cocktail parties for sensational food. Once I timidly asked her for some recipes, and have used them ever since. This is one of them. Thanks, Nancy Paine, wherever you are!

Makes 60 bite-size rolls

Salads & Dressings

When we first bought the inn, I had no intention of spending much time in the kitchen. I'd raised five children, gone back to school, and worked hard to get out of the kitchen. However, there was this little problem: the inn's cook had just run away.

T.C.

J & J's Basil Cream Dressing

Whenever possible, use fresh basil for this dressing. Dried basil works well, but is not nearly as pungent and aromatic.

1 clove garlic, minced
2 tablespoons chopped parsley
¼ cup white wine vinegar
2 tablespoons Dijon mustard
1 egg
⅔ cup vegetable oil
4 to 6 tablespoons fresh minced basil
   or 3 to 4 tablespoons dried
Dash of sugar
Salt and freshly ground pepper to taste

Place garlic, parsley, vinegar, mustard, and the egg into the bowl of a food processor. Mix well. With the processor running, add the vegetable oil in a slow, steady stream and process until smooth and thickened.

Stop the machine for a minute to add the basil, sugar, salt, and pepper. Process briefly until blended. Taste and correct the seasoning as needed. To serve, spoon over a mixed garden salad and enjoy!

Makes 1 cup

During my first year at the inn, I promised to do a large buffet for a summer wedding reception. The bride wanted a variety of salads, and I desperately wanted ideas for at least one unusual dressing. Prior to the wedding we had a cooking class in progress. Two of the students, Jean True and Julie Wolski, were professional caterers from Chicago. What luck! "Dressing?" they mused when I asked them. "Sure, we know a great dressing." Just one little hitch: they didn't have the recipe. No matter. They just collected the ingredients, grabbed the food processor, pad, and pen, and for the next twenty minutes talked, laughed, measured, tasted, frowned, mixed, retasted, whispered, smiled, wrote, and finally grinned with satisfaction: the dressing had been re-created, just the way they remembered it.

Naturally, I used it at the wedding, with great success, and still use it for our inn guests in the summer when fresh basil abounds in our herb garden. Jean and Julie, thanks again!

Omi's Basic Vinaigrette

1 tablespoon Dijon mustard
½ teaspoon salt
¼ teaspoon pepper
1 tablespoon plus 1 teaspoon sugar
3 tablespoons rice vinegar or white vinegar
  (rice vinegar is better)
6 tablespoons water
3 tablespoons vegetable oil
2 tablespoons minced red onion (or scallions
  or chives)
1 tablespoon minced parsley

In a small bowl, whisk the mustard with the
salt, pepper, and sugar. Add the vinegar and
water. Mix well. Slowly add the oil, then whisk
vigorously. Add the onion and parsley. Mix well
and correct the taste: the dressing should have a
mild sweet-and-sour flavor.

Pour dressing over
salad, toss, and serve.

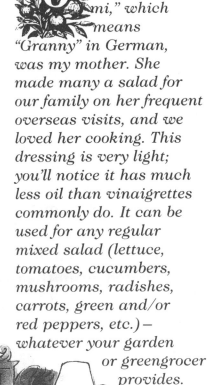

"Omi," which
means
"Granny" in German,
was my mother. She
made many a salad for
our family on her frequent
overseas visits, and we
loved her cooking. This
dressing is very light;
you'll notice it has much
less oil than vinaigrettes
commonly do. It can be
used for any regular
mixed salad (lettuce,
tomatoes, cucumbers,
mushrooms, radishes,
carrots, green and/or
red peppers, etc.)—
whatever your garden
or greengrocer
provides.

Makes ⅔ cup

Poppy Seed Dressing with Honey and Bourbon

1 cup Dijon mustard
¾ cup red wine vinegar
¾ cup honey
½ cup bourbon
1½ cups vegetable oil
2 tablespoons poppy seeds

In a bowl, whisk mustard, vinegar, honey, and bourbon. Gradually add the oil, whisking vigorously until well blended. When the dressing no longer separates, mix in the poppy seeds.

Use what you need and store the rest in a tightly covered jar in the refrigerator. Keeps for weeks . . . maybe forever!

One of our favorite dressings for regular mixed garden salads. Our guests love it and frequently ask for the recipe.

Makes 3 cups

Jicama and Green Bean Salad
with Sesame Dressing

Salad

1 large jicama (Mexican root vegetable)
1 pound fresh green beans (young thin ones are best)
½ red pepper for garnish (or use firm tomato strips or cherry tomato halves)

Dressing

2 tablespoons rice wine vinegar
1 tablespoon water
1 teaspoon sugar
2 teaspoons sesame oil
Salt and freshly ground pepper to taste
1 tablespoon sesame seeds

 *This excellent green-white-red salad, based on a recipe from Steven Raichlen's cooking class, looks beautiful and has a mild oriental flavor. All the ingredients should be readily available at any good supermarket.*

Peel the jicama with a paring knife and cut it into strips the size of thin French fries. Snap or cut the ends off the beans. Drop the beans into rapidly boiling water and boil for only 3 minutes. Drain and drop them into a bowl of cold water to stop the cooking and preserve the color. Drain and set aside. Remove any white membrane and seeds from the inside of the red pepper. Using a sharp paring knife, cut the pepper into ¼-inch strips, and cut those into triangles. Set aside.

Place the vinegar, water, sugar, and oil in a small bowl and whisk to mix. Add salt and pepper to taste. Correct the seasoning: the dressing should have a nice balance of sweet and sour. Set aside.

In a small frying pan, toast the sesame seeds to a golden color. Let cool and set aside (salad can be done 24 hours ahead of time up to this stage; just keep everything covered and refrigerated).

To assemble, toss the jicama and beans with the dressing and place on individual salad plates. Sprinkle with pepper triangles and sesame seeds. Serve at once.

Serves 4

Tortellini Salad

Dressing

⅓ cup red wine vinegar
⅓ cup vegetable oil
⅓ cup olive oil
½ cup thinly sliced green onions
3 tablespoons minced parsley
2 cloves garlic, minced
4 teaspoons fresh minced basil or 2 teaspoons dried
2 teaspoons fresh minced dill or 1 teaspoon dried
1 teaspoon fresh minced oregano or ½ teaspoon dried
½ teaspoon pepper
½ teaspoon sugar
1½ teaspoons Dijon mustard
1 teaspoon salt or to taste

Combine all ingredients (except the salt) in a jar and cover tightly. Shake vigorously until well mixed. Add additional salt if needed. Set aside.

Salad

12 ounces cheese-stuffed tortellini, uncooked
2 cups fresh snow peas
2 cups fresh broccoli florets
2 cups sliced mushrooms
1 14-ounce can pitted black olives, drained
2 tablespoons freshly grated Parmesan cheese
2 cups cherry tomatoes, cut in halves

Cook the tortellini according to package directions. Drain and cool. Place in a big bowl, add the salad dressing, mix, and set aside.

Colorful vegetables, cheese-stuffed tortellini, and a dressing rich with herbs make this version of a pasta salad our favorite. It can be made ahead; in fact it tastes best when allowed to marinate overnight.

Blanch the green vegetables: drop the snow peas in boiling water and cook for 30 seconds. Remove them with a slotted spoon or strainer. Immediately drop them into a bowl of cold water. Drain again and set aside. Do the same with the broccoli but boil for 1 minute. Blanching makes the vegetables more tender and intensifies their color.

Add snow peas, broccoli, mushrooms, olives, and 1 tablespoon Parmesan to the tortellini. Mix well. Chill for several hours or overnight. Add the tomatoes last. Sprinkle the top of the salad with 1 tablespoon of Parmesan and serve.

Serves 12

Rice Salad with Chicken and Pears

Salad

1 large whole chicken breast, skinned and boned
2 cups chicken stock
3 cups white rice, cooked and cooled
1 cup wild rice, cooked and cooled
1 cup chopped celery
4 scallions, washed and chopped into ¼-inch
    rings
3 ripe but firm pears
Zest and juice of 1 lemon
Enough dressing to bind (see below)
1 tablespoon fresh minced parsley

This hearty salad makes excellent picnic fare. Just be sure it's well chilled and carried in a cooler to prevent spoilage.

Heat the chicken stock, place the chicken in it and simmer, partially covered, for 5 to 8 minutes or until tender. Drain and cool. Cut into ½-inch cubes and set aside.

Lightly toss white and wild rice, celery, scallions, chicken, and lemon zest in a large bowl. Core, quarter, and thinly slice the pears. Immediately drizzle them with lemon juice to keep them from discoloring. Toss to coat well. Add them to the rice salad.

Dressing

1 cup good mayonnaise
1 cup sour cream
⅓ cup mango chutney
1 tablespoon Tamari soy sauce
1 tablespoon Dijon mustard
Salt and pepper to taste

$\mathcal{P}$lace mayonnaise, sour cream, chutney, Tamari, and mustard in food processor. Process for 1 minute. Season with salt and pepper to taste, process briefly, and correct the seasoning if necessary.

$\mathcal{A}$dd the dressing, just enough to bind the salad (store whatever dressing is left in a tightly covered jar in the refrigerator). Mix well and chill the salad for at least 4 hours. Serve garnished with minced parsley.

$\mathcal{S}$erves 6

# Spinach Salad with Oranges and Mint

1 pound fresh spinach
2 navel oranges
⅓ cup extra virgin olive oil
2 tablespoons orange juice
1 tablespoon balsamic vinegar
Salt and pepper to taste
½ cup fresh mint leaves
3 strawberries (optional)

Stem, rinse, and spin dry the spinach. Tear into bite-size pieces. Divide between 6 individual salad plates.

Peel the orange and cut into ½-inch chunks. Sprinkle them on top of the spinach.

In a small bowl, whisk the oil, orange juice, vinegar, salt, and pepper (careful with the salt, you need just a little) until well blended. Add the mint leaves. Taste and correct the seasoning.

Spoon dressing over each salad, garnish with half of a strawberry, and serve at once.

A light, refreshing salad, especially nice in the summer when both spinach and mint are plentiful.

Serves 4 to 6

Soups

*Blessed with more guts than brains, I decided
to tackle the job of cooking for the inn until we found
a good chef — two months, maybe three at the most.
I didn't figure on getting hooked.*

T.C.

Sherried Parsnip Soup

4 tablespoons butter
1 bunch parsnips (about 1 pound), chopped
2 large carrots, chopped
2 large onions, chopped
3 cups chicken stock
2 cups heavy cream
Salt and pepper to taste
2 tablespoons dry sherry
2 tablespoons minced parsley

Aroma, color, and flavor; this soup has it all!

Melt the butter and sauté parsnips, carrots, and onions for about 20 minutes or until soft. Add just enough chicken stock to cover, and simmer another 30 minutes.

Purée vegetables in blender or food processor. Return to stove and reheat, adding cream and the rest of the chicken stock. Salt and pepper to taste. Add the sherry shortly before serving.

Sprinkle with parsley and serve.

Serves 8

 Danish Crab Soup

4 tablespoons butter
1 large onion, chopped
2 leeks, rinsed well and chopped
2 carrots, scrubbed and shredded
1 teaspoon curry powder
4 medium potatoes, peeled and chopped
9-ounce fish filet (haddock, salmon, sole, or any boned fish), chopped
4 to 6 ounces crabmeat
Salt and pepper to taste
1 cup dry white wine
½ cup sour cream
⅓ cup minced parsley

Melt the butter and sauté onions for 10 minutes. Add the leeks, carrots, and curry powder and sauté another 10 minutes. Add the potatoes, fish, and 2 cups water. Bring to a boil, then simmer until the potatoes are soft. Cool slightly.

Process this mixture in a food processor until creamy smooth. Return mixture to a pot. Add the crabmeat and 2 cups *boiling* water. Cover and let the soup steep for 5 minutes.

Reheat the soup, adding salt, pepper, wine, and parsley. Correct the seasoning to taste. Remove from heat and whisk in sour cream. Garnish with parsley (or green scallion rings, croutons, or chives) and serve at once.

Serves 8

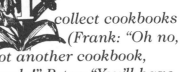 *collect cookbooks (Frank: "Oh no, not another cookbook, Trudy!" Peter: "You'll have to pay for this one yourself, Mom!" So much for support). But my mother collected recipes, bought notebooks, tabbed the pages by categories, and handwrote them all. Going through her things after her death, I found several of those notebooks and they are some of my greatest treasures.*

I'm just beginning to test a few of her dishes. Some I remember from my childhood, some are new. Mother's Danish crab soup, a lighthearted parallel to the robust New England fish chowder, turned out to be a winner with our guests.

Tomato Cognac Soup

1 large Spanish onion
3 ounces butter
3 pounds canned, peeled plum tomatoes
1 tablespoon dried basil
1 pint heavy or all-purpose cream
1 to 2 tablespoons dark brown sugar
5 tablespoons cognac
Salt and pepper to taste
Minced parsley for garnish

Chop the onion and sauté in butter for 20 minutes until soft and translucent but not brown. With your fingers, squash the tomatoes; add them and all the liquid in the can to the onion. Add the basil and stir. Bring the soup to a boil, then simmer, covered, for 30 minutes. Set aside and cool slightly, then purée the soup in a food processor.

In a small saucepan heat the cream with the sugar, whisking often. Pour this mixture into the soup. Reheat, but do not boil.

Just before serving, add the cognac and season with salt and pepper. Garnish with parsley and serve. Just great!

No doubt, this is one of our most popular soups and an honored classic. We got the recipe from the previous innkeepers, the Blymeyers, who got it out of a vegetarian cookbook, and who knows where those authors got it. In any case, it is here to stay, a solid part of our repertoire. Like all classics, it is tasteful, elegant, and simple.

Serves 6

Maple Butternut Bisque

3 ounces butter
2 cups chopped onion
¼ cup flour
1½ cups milk
3 cups chicken stock
3 pounds canned butternut squash
Dash of cayenne pepper
Salt to taste
¾ cup heavy cream
¼ cup maple syrup
Toasted and chopped pecans for garnish

This soup features a wonderfully unusual blend of flavors, perfect for chilly fall and winter meals.

Melt the butter and sauté the onion until soft and translucent, about 20 minutes. Sprinkle flour over the onions and cook for 2 or 3 more minutes. Slowly add the milk and cook, stirring constantly. Add the chicken stock and squash. Mix well and bring to a boil. Lower the heat and simmer for 10 minutes, stirring often. Season with cayenne pepper and salt.

Add the cream and maple syrup. Blend well. Let simmer for a few minutes longer. Correct the taste, if needed, with a bit more seasoning and/or syrup. Serve hot, garnished with a sprinkling of toasted pecans.

Serves 8

Spargelcremesuppe
(Asparagus Cream Soup)

1½ pounds fresh asparagus, trimmed of woody
    ends and washed well
½ teaspoon salt
3 pints chicken stock
5 tablespoons butter
4 tablespoons flour
1 cup heavy cream, mixed with 1 egg yolk
Salt and pepper to taste
Dash of ground nutmeg
Minced parsley for garnish

Simmer asparagus in 2 cups salted water until
tender. Drain, but save the broth. Cut off tips and
set aside. Chop the rest of the asparagus and
purée in the food processor or blender.

Transfer purée to a large saucepan. Whisk in
the chicken stock and simmer for 10 minutes. In
a separate pot, heat the saved asparagus broth.

Make a roux: melt butter, stir in the flour, and
cook for 2 minutes, stirring often. Slowly mix in
the hot broth, stirring vigorously to prevent
clumping. When very smooth, whisk mixture into
the purée. Bring the soup to a boil and simmer
for 10 minutes.

Remove the soup from heat. Whisk in the
cream/yolk mixture. Add salt, pepper, and
nutmeg. Correct the taste to your liking. Serve
garnished with parsley and the reserved
asparagus tips.

Serves 6

This is a great Austrian soup using one of spring's first vegetables. You can use canned asparagus, but fresh is best!

Potato Leek Soup

4 strips bacon
1 medium onion, chopped
3 leeks, washed and chopped
4 medium potatoes, peeled and chopped
6 cups chicken stock
Salt and pepper to taste
Minced parsley or chives for garnish

Fry the bacon, drain it between paper towels, and dice it. In the same frying pan, use the rendered bacon fat to sauté the onions for 10 minutes. Add the leeks, then sauté another 5 minutes or until onions and leeks are soft. Add potatoes and just enough chicken stock to cover. Bring to a boil, then simmer until potatoes are soft. Stir often.

Remove the soup from the stove and let it cool slightly. Purée in food processor, adding more chicken stock if needed.

Reheat the soup. Add the rest of the chicken stock. Soup should be creamy thick, not runny. Add three-quarters of the bacon, stir well, and adjust the taste with salt and pepper.

Serve piping hot, garnished with the rest of the bacon and parsley (or chives or green onion rings).

Serves 6

A wonderfully hearty winter soup from my mother's kitchen. No matter how cold the day, this will warm you up!

 Dilled Mushroom Soup

 *Even if you hate mushrooms, you'll love this soup!*

2 tablespoons butter
2 cups chopped onion
1 pound mushrooms, rinsed and chopped;
   reserve 1 or 2 nice ones to slice for garnish
2 tablespoons fresh minced dill
1 tablespoon Tamari soy sauce
1½ tablespoons paprika
½ to 1 cup chicken stock

1 tablespoon butter
3 tablespoons flour
1 cup milk

1 to 2 tablespoons lemon juice
Salt and pepper to taste
Fresh dill sprigs for garnish

Sauté the onion in 2 tablespoons butter for
20 minutes or until soft. Add mushrooms, dill,
Tamari, and paprika. Stir. Add just enough of the
chicken stock to barely cover the vegetables.
Cover and simmer for 20 minutes.

Make a roux: in a sauce pan, melt 1 tablespoon
butter, then whisk in the flour. Cook and stir for
5 minutes, then add the milk. Stirring constantly,
cook this until the roux has thickened. Pour into
the soup and blend. Add more stock if needed.
Cover and simmer for about 15 minutes.

For final seasoning, add the lemon juice and
salt and pepper to taste. Garnish each serving
with a sprig of dill and a thin slice of mushroom.

Serves 6

Dilled Cream of Cucumber Soup

A great summer soup when cucumbers are at their cheapest and most flavorful.

3 tablespoons butter
1 cup chopped onion
3 cucumbers, peeled, seeded, and chopped
3 cups chicken stock
1 cup water
1 cup heavy cream
3 tablespoons fresh minced dill; chop and
  reserve all stems
Salt and pepper to taste

*I*n a saucepan, melt the butter. Add the onion and sauté 10 minutes. Peel the cucumbers and cut in half lengthwise. Scoop out the seeds and discard. Roughly chop 2½ of the cucumbers, setting one half aside. Add the chopped cucumbers to the onion. Add 1 cup of the stock, water, and chopped dill stems. Simmer, covered, for 30 minutes until cucumbers are very soft.

*C*hop the remaining cucumber into small (¼-inch or so) cubes and simmer in lightly salted water for 20 minutes. Refresh in cold water, drain, and set aside.

*P*urée the soup in a food processor to creamy consistency. Return to pot and reheat, adding the rest of the stock, the cream, and most of the minced dill. Correct the taste with salt and pepper if necessary. Stir in reserved cucumber cubes.

*G*arnish with the rest of the dill and serve.

*S*erves 6

If you ever go to Salzburg, Austria, my hometown, make sure you have dinner at the Oesterreichische Hof. Whenever I visit, my family takes me to dinner there. Since dinner in Austria is "Mittagessen," or lunch, your table by the window isn't wasted — you look out across the river to the ancient city and the castle above. The food is as fabulous as the view, and it's easy to get the itch to go backstage. Prior to my last visit I wrote to the hotel management, and they graciously agreed to let me look into the pots. For three mornings I scooted around the huge two-story kitchen, equipped with pad, pen, and camera — what fun! This Gurkensuppe is one of the many souvenirs I brought back.

Minted Green Soup

4 tablespoons butter
2 cups chopped onion
10 ounces frozen spinach
10 ounces frozen peas
2½ to 3 cups chicken stock
½ cup fresh mint leaves or 2 tablespoons dried
2 tablespoons fresh marjoram leaves
    or 1 teaspoon dried
1 cup heavy cream
Salt and pepper to taste
Diced red pepper for garnish

Melt the butter and sauté the onion for about 20 minutes. Add the defrosted spinach and peas and just enough chicken stock (approximately 2 cups) to cover the vegetables. Add the mint and marjoram and stir well. Bring to a boil and simmer for 2 minutes—no longer, or the fresh green color will turn to khaki. Remove the soup from the heat and let it cool for about 15 minutes.

Using a food processor, purée the soup to a smooth, creamy texture. Return to the stove and reheat. Add the cream and, if necessary, thin out with a bit more chicken stock. Add salt and pepper. Check and correct the taste.

Serve, sprinkled with a bit of diced red pepper. Soup should be just thick enough to float the garnish.

Here's another summery soup that's pleasing to both the eye and the palate.

Serves 6 to 8

Chilled Cherry Soup

This is a glorious hot-summer-night soup. Serve small portions in champagne glasses as an elegant overture to a light dinner.

2 pounds fresh cherries*
½ cup sugar
1 cinnamon stick
2 allspice berries
2 whole cloves
3 black peppercorns
2 strips lemon peel
Pinch of salt
1 tablespoon cornstarch
½ cup heavy cream
¾ cup dry red wine
Sour cream or yogurt for garnish

Pit the cherries and save their juice. To the cherry juice, add enough water to make a total of 3 cups of liquid and put that in a saucepan. Add the sugar and cinnamon stick. Add allspice, cloves, and peppercorns wrapped in a piece of cheesecloth. Add the lemon peel and salt and bring the soup to a boil. Add the cherries and simmer for 15 minutes.

Dissolve the cornstarch in 2 tablespoons cold water and stir into the soup. Boil for 1 minute to thicken slightly. Cool the soup to room temperature, then chill for at least 4 hours or overnight.

Shortly before serving, remove the cinnamon stick and spice bag, and mix in the cream and wine. Serve garnished with a dollop of sour cream or yogurt.

Restaurant critic and food writer Steven Raichlen, who occasionally teaches cooking classes at this inn, introduced me to this soup. He couldn't believe I'd never heard of cold cherry soup, supposedly an Austro-Hungarian classic. Well, I hadn't. When it comes to food, little Austria is a big country: it's made a habit of appropriating the best recipes from the seven surrounding nations.

But as I dreamily ladled my third helping, a childhood memory floated up from that fragrant bowl . . . a balmy summer evening out on the terrace . . . swallows slashing a sky steeped in lingering dusk . . . my mother proudly serving this special cold soup . . . and what did my father say? "Next time, Lisl, I want hot Nudelsuppe."

I wish he could have tasted this one.

Serves 8   *If using canned cherries, omit the sugar and add the cherries last.

Breads & Muffins

The bread recipes in this section use all-purpose white flour unless otherwise indicated.

What if my food wasn't up to the guests' expectations? Thoughts like that made me sit bolt upright in bed at two in the morning wondering if I should just run away to Greece and start a new life.

T.C.

Cottage Cheese Onion Bread

3 packages dry yeast
¾ cup warm water
3 tablespoons sugar

3 cups cottage cheese
1 teaspoon salt
¾ teaspoon baking soda
⅓ cup butter, softened
3 eggs
1 or 2 packages onion soup mix (to taste)
8 to 9 cups flour

Moist and super-savory!

Sprinkle yeast on ¾ cup warm water. Add sugar and stir until dissolved. Let stand for 10 minutes to activate yeast.

In a large bowl, combine the cheese, salt, baking soda, butter, eggs, and soup mix (use 2 packages if you prefer a strong onion flavor). Stir to blend. Add the yeast mixture. Stir in 4 cups flour and blend well. Stir in enough remaining flour to make a stiff dough.

Turn dough onto a lightly floured surface and knead thoroughly. Grease a bowl with melted butter. Place dough in bowl, turning to coat all over. Cover and let rise in a warm, draft-free place until double in size.

Turn out onto lightly floured surface again and knead gently to deflate. Divide dough into 2 equal pieces, cover, and let rise for 10 minutes. Then shape into 2 loaves and place in buttered loaf pans. Cover and let rise until doubled.

Preheat oven to 350° and bake for 40 to 45 minutes or until browned and done.

Makes 2 loaves

Challah Bread

2 packages dry yeast
1⅓ cups warm water
1 tablespoon sugar

1 tablespoon coarse salt
3 tablespoons soft butter
3 eggs
5½ cups flour
1 egg yolk mixed with 1 teaspoon cold water
Poppy seeds

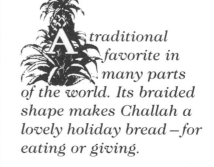

A traditional favorite in many parts of the world. Its braided shape makes Challah a lovely holiday bread—for eating or giving.

In a large bowl, sprinkle the yeast and sugar on the warm water. When bubbly, add salt, butter, eggs, and 5 cups flour, one cup at a time. Beat thoroughly with a wooden spoon. Gradually add more flour until dough is very stiff.

Turn dough out onto a board dusted with flour. Knead until smooth and silky, for about 10 minutes. Place dough in a large buttered bowl, turning to coat with butter; cover and let rise in a warm place until double in bulk, about 2 hours.

Punch down and divide into 6 equal parts. Roll each portion into a rope 1 inch thick. Braid 3 ropes to make one loaf, then the other 3 for the second. Carefully transfer the two loaves to a buttered baking sheet, cover, and let rise in a warm place until double in size.

Preheat oven to 400°. Brush loaves with the egg wash and sprinkle with poppy seeds. Bake for 35 to 40 minutes. Cool on racks.

Makes 2 loaves

 Beer Bread

12 ounces of beer (any kind, light or dark)
⅔ cup molasses
2 cups hot water
1 package dry yeast

4¼ cups rye flour
2½ teaspoons salt
4¼ cups white flour
Melted butter

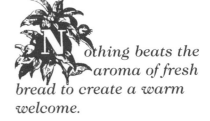

Nothing beats the aroma of fresh bread to create a warm welcome.

In a large bowl, mix the beer, molasses, and water. Sprinkle yeast on this mixture and leave in a warm place for 10 minutes to activate the yeast.

Stir in the rye flour and salt. Mix well, cover, and let rest for 30 minutes.

Gradually stir in the white flour. When dough becomes too unwieldy, empty onto a flat surface and work in the rest of the flour by kneading vigorously. Return dough to bowl and cover with a warm, damp towel. Move to a warm place and let dough rise until double in bulk (about 2 hours).

Turn dough onto floured flat surface and knead, adding extra white flour if needed. Knead until dough is smooth and springy. With a knife, divide dough into 4 equal parts. Shape each one into a ball and place on buttered baking sheet.

Preheat oven to 400°. Brush the loaves well all over with the melted butter and bake for 10 minutes. Reduce heat to 350° and bake 20 to 25 minutes more. Remove from the oven and cool before slicing.

Makes 4 round loaves

 Oatmeal Sesame Bread

5 cups milk
5 tablespoons butter
5 tablespoons honey
5 teaspoons salt
3 packages dry yeast
12 cups flour
3 cups oatmeal
1 cup sesame seeds
1 egg, slightly beaten
Sesame seeds for garnish

Scald the milk, then add the butter, honey, and salt. Set aside and let cool to just warm.

Dissolve the yeast in 1 cup warm water. Let stand for 10 minutes.

Pour the milk/honey mix into a large bowl and add the yeast mixture. Add the flour, oatmeal, and sesame seeds. Mix well. Turn dough onto a lightly floured surface and knead until smooth and satiny. Place dough in a greased bowl, turning to coat all over. Cover and let rise in a warm, draft-free place until double in size.

Turn the dough out and knead gently to deflate. Divide into 4 equal parts and place in greased loaf pans. Cover and let rise until double in size.

Preheat oven to 350° and bake the breads for 1 hour or until golden brown and done.

Remove from pans and let loaves cool on rack. While still warm, brush with egg and sprinkle with sesame seeds.

Makes 4 large loaves

This recipe is a contribution from Jane Ross, who lives nearby and likes to keep books and read stars. Her recipe is as precise as it is heavenly.

Oatmeal Bread

2 cups water
1 tablespoon butter
½ cup molasses
1 cup oatmeal

4 to 5 cups flour
1 tablespoon salt
2 packages dry yeast

A robust dark bread that's really easy to make.

In a saucepan, warm the water, butter, molasses, and oatmeal. Mix the flour, salt, and yeast in a large bowl, then add the oatmeal mixture and blend well. Turn dough onto a lightly floured board and knead for 10 minutes. Transfer dough to a greased bowl, brush the top with butter, cover lightly, and let rise in a warm place until double in size.

Punch down and divide in half. Form 2 loaves and place each in a greased loaf pan, cover, and let rise for about 1 hour.

Preheat oven to 350° and bake the loaves for 30 minutes. Cool before slicing.

Makes 2 loaves

Buttermilk Honey Bread

1 package dry yeast
1 teaspoon honey
¾ cup warm water

2 tablespoons unsalted butter, softened
3 tablespoons honey
5¾ to 6¼ cups flour
1 tablespoon salt
1½ cups buttermilk, lukewarm

Buttermilk and honey add old-fashioned appeal to this bread.

Sprinkle the dry yeast on ¾ cup of warm water. Add the honey and stir to dissolve. Let stand for 10 minutes to activate yeast.

In a large bowl, stir the butter with 3 tablespoons honey. Add 2 cups flour, the salt, and buttermilk. Add yeast mixture and stir until smooth. Using a wooden spoon, add the remaining flour, ½ cup at a time, then turn dough onto a floured surface and knead until smooth and satiny, about 10 minutes. If the dough is still sticky, add more flour.

Grease a large bowl. Place the dough in it, turning to coat entire surface. Cover the bowl with plastic wrap and let the dough rise in a warm, draft-free place until double in size, about 2 hours.

Grease two baking sheets. Gently knead dough on lightly floured surface until deflated. Cut in half. Knead each piece into a round shape, then pull opposite sides under to form an oval. Place on baking sheet, seam side down. Cover with a towel and let rise in a warm, draft-free place until double in size, about 45 minutes.

Preheat oven to 375° and bake for 45 minutes or until brown and hollow-sounding when tapped on bottom. Let cool before slicing.

Makes 2 loaves

Russian Black Bread

2 cups water
¼ cup molasses
¼ cup cider vinegar
¼ cup (½ stick) unsalted butter
1 ounce unsweetened chocolate
2 teaspoons instant coffee

Combine the above ingredients in a small saucepan. Heat until the butter is melted. Set aside to cool.

½ cup warm water
4 tablespoons dry yeast
1 tablespoon sugar
3 cups unbleached flour
3 cups rye flour
½ cup whole wheat flour
1 cup unprocessed bran
2 tablespoons caraway seeds
1 teaspoon fennel seeds
2 tablespoons salt
2 tablespoons minced onion

Sprinkle yeast and sugar on water, mix to suspend yeast, and let stand for 10 minutes in a warm place to proof.

Measure out on a pastry board or counter the remaining ingredients and blend. Make a "well" in the center. Add the cooled molasses mixture and the yeast, working in the flour as you go. Knead the dough until smooth, about 10 minutes. Turn into a large bowl, cover, and let rise in a warm place for at least 1 hour or until double in size.

Punch down. Form bread into loaves. Preheat oven to 350°. Bake for about 40 minutes.

Makes 2 average or 6 small loaves

The Russian answer to German pumpernickel, this substantial bread goes especially well with a hearty winter meal. Great with cheese fondue, too.

Peasant Bread

4 cups warm water
2 tablespoons yeast
1 teaspoon sugar
9½ cups flour
2 tablespoons salt
1 egg, slightly beaten
Sesame or other seeds

In a large bowl, combine warm water, yeast, and sugar and let stand 10 minutes to "proof" the yeast. Add 4 cups flour and salt. Mix and beat for 2 minutes, then let the dough rest and "sponge" for 15 minutes.

Gradually add 5½ cups flour. Knead until the dough is smooth. If you use an electric dough hook, the dough should clean the bowl.

Cover the bowl and place it in a warm, draft-free place. Let the dough rise until double in size. Punch down and turn it out onto a floured surface. Form 2 loaves, place in buttered bread pans, cover, and let rise. Preheat oven to 375°. Bake for 30 minutes or until done.

While still warm, brush the loaves with egg and sprinkle with seeds.

Makes 2 loaves

Peasant bread, like French bread, has no shortening and tastes best when fresh; it doesn't freeze well. But to me there is nothing like a buttered slice from a loaf still warm from the oven. Short of real San Francisco sourdough, it's better than any dessert.

Sour Cream Bread

1 package dry yeast
3 tablespoons sugar
¼ cup warm water
2 cups sour cream, room temperature
1 tablespoon salt
1 teaspoon baking soda
4½ to 5 cups flour

Combine yeast, sugar, and water. Allow to proof 5 minutes.

In a large bowl, mix sour cream with salt and baking soda. Add the yeast mixture, then 4 cups flour, 1 cup at a time, to make a sticky, wet dough. Beat hard with a wooden spoon.

Scrape the dough onto a lightly floured board and knead for about 10 minutes, adding only enough flour to prevent sticking. Shape dough into a ball and place in a buttered bowl. Turn to coat with butter and cover with plastic wrap. Place in a warm, draft-free spot. Let rise until double in size.

Punch down. Turn out onto a lightly floured board and knead 1 minute more. Divide evenly in half and shape 2 loaves. Place them in greased 9 x 5 x 3 loaf tins. Cover and let rise until double in size.

Preheat oven to 375°. Bake for 30 to 35 minutes. Cool before slicing.

Makes 2 large loaves

Not quite like sourdough, but moist and wonderfully tangy!

Pumpkin Bread

5 cups flour
1 cup light brown sugar
3 cups sugar
3 teaspoons baking soda
1 tablespoon ground cloves
1 tablespoon ground cinnamon
1½ teaspoons ground nutmeg
1 tablespoon rum
1 cup cooking oil
1 29-ounce can pumpkin
2 cups chopped walnuts

Preheat oven to 325°. Thoroughly grease 3 loaf pans.

In a large bowl, mix the flour, sugars, baking soda, and spices. In another bowl, mix the rum, oil, pumpkin, and nuts. Add the wet mix to the dry and blend well. Turn evenly into the 3 loaf pans and bake for 1½ hours or until done (test with a toothpick).

Remove from pans and let cool on racks. While still warm, dust with powdered sugar.

Makes 3 loaves

A great make-ahead-and-freeze bread for Thanksgiving or Christmas.

Banana Bread

¼ cup butter, softened
¾ cup sugar
1 egg
3 very ripe bananas, mashed
1½ cups flour
1 teaspoon soda
¼ teaspoon salt
Powdered sugar

Cream the butter with the sugar and egg until smooth and fluffy. Add the mashed bananas and blend.

Mix the flour with the baking soda and salt. Add to the banana mixture and stir well.

Preheat oven to 350°. Grease a loaf pan and fill it with the banana dough. Bake for 45 minutes or until done (test with a toothpick). Sift some powdered sugar over the top while still warm.

Delicious with your morning coffee!

Makes 1 loaf

Buttermilk Muffins

Preheat oven to 400°. Grease the muffin tins (a spray works best). In a large bowl, place the following dry ingredients:

4 cups flour
⅔ cup sugar
2 tablespoons baking powder
1 teaspoon salt

Blend and set aside. In another, smaller bowl mix the following wet ingredients:

2 eggs
1 cup cooking oil
2⅓ cups buttermilk

Add the wet mixture to the dry ingredients and mix until just blended. Do not overmix unless you like cementlike pancakes instead of fluffy muffins!

Fill muffin cups no more than two-thirds to three-quarters full and bake at 400° for 18 to 20 minutes. Enjoy them still warm from the oven, with a bit of butter.

Another basic muffin recipe but made with buttermilk. A cup of fruit — chopped apples, pears, blueberries, cherries, raisins — can be added to the wet mix to make these muffins even more delicious.

Makes about 2 to 2½ dozen

Snowvillage Inn Morning Muffins

2 cups flour
2 teaspoons baking powder
1 teaspoon salt
1 cup sugar
½ cup milk
½ cup sour cream
¼ cup cooking oil
1 egg
1 cup chopped fruit: apples, peaches,
  blueberries, pears, pineapple, dates –
  you name it

Generously grease or spray a muffin tin.
Preheat oven to 400°.

In one bowl, mix the dry ingredients (flour,
baking powder, salt, and sugar). In another bowl,
mix the wet ingredients (milk, sour cream, oil,
and egg).

Add the wet mix to the dry ingredients and stir
in the fruit. Do not overmix. Spoon into the tins
and bake for 20 minutes or until golden brown.
Serve warm with sweet butter. Yum!

Makes 9 large muffins

Our basic muffin, freshly baked each morning and served right out of the oven. There is no better companion to that first cup of coffee!

Leslie's Blueberry Cinnamon Muffins

Preheat the oven to 375°. Grease the muffin pan with butter or cooking spray.

In one bowl, blend the liquids:

1 egg, lightly beaten
2 tablespoons soft butter or vegetable oil
¾ cup milk

In another bowl, blend the solids:

½ cup sugar
1 cup flour
1 teaspoon baking powder
½ teaspoon ground cinnamon
¼ teaspoon ground cloves
½ teaspoon salt
1½ cups fresh or frozen wild blueberries
   (if frozen, drain well)

In a small cup, mix the topping:

2 tablespoons sugar
1 teaspoon ground cinnamon

Add the liquids to the solids and quickly blend the ingredients with a rubber spatula. Do not overmix. Fill the muffin cups, sprinkle with the topping, and bake for 20 to 25 minutes. Have some sweet butter and a mug of coffee ready — you're in for a glorious morning!

Makes 8 muffins

After one year of innkeeping and doing most of the cooking day after day, I realized I needed help, or I might answer those want ads and go off to teach English in Japan or join the Peace Corps . . . early signs of burnout. Steve Raichlen told me about a former student in one of his cooking classes, Leslie Russell, who lived close by. She agreed to come for an interview. When I first saw her, I thought no woman with gray hair has the right to look so slim, young, and happy. On top of that, two minutes into the interview, she laughed, showing strong, perfect teeth. I could hate her or be inspired. We hired the inspiration.

But it wasn't until the night the propane gas ran out and she could laugh about that — and deal with it — that we became friends. What cook do you know who seasons food with laughter?

Leslie, who grew up in New England, fondly remembers those lazy summer mornings of her childhood when she'd wake up to the teasing aroma of just-baked muffins loaded with fresh wild blueberries, their special flavor enhanced with cinnamon and just a touch of clove. Our recipe is based on one from her mother.

Vegetables

Liz, a caterer who had started out as a cook at this inn, came over to teach me. I watched her take a red pepper, cradle it in her hand like a bird, and explain how she would use it for a garnish. That's all. But she smiled and sparkled and enjoyed herself, and some of that joy seemed to flow into her hands, the way she held that pepper, that knife. That pepper wasn't just a pepper anymore, but something gorgeous and important, transforming itself under her expert knife into crimson jewels to be scattered, later, over the emerald of steamed broccoli. This was something I wanted to do; this could be fun!

T.C.

Broccoli with Cherry Tomatoes and Basil

1 large head broccoli
12 cherry tomatoes
4 tablespoons butter
½ teaspoon dried basil (or 1 tablespoon chopped
　　fresh)
Salt and pepper to taste

Cut the broccoli into florets. Cut the upper part of the stem into thin slices. Boil a large pot of salted water, about 1 teaspoon salt per quart. Add the stem slices and boil for 2 minutes. Add the florets and boil for 3 minutes more. Drain in a colander and immediately immerse the broccoli in a large container of cold water to retain color and crispness.

Melt 1 tablespoon butter in a small frying pan. Add basil and sauté for 30 seconds. Add the cherry tomatoes, sprinkle with salt and pepper, sauté and toss lightly, about 2 minutes. Tomatoes should be hot but not mushy.

Melt the rest of the butter in a large frying pan. Using a sieve, briefly dip the broccoli in boiling water to reheat. Gently decant into the frying pan and sprinkle with salt and pepper. Toss lightly with the tomatoes and serve at once, using 2 cherry tomatoes per serving.

Simple but elegant, and a colorful, savory dish for the holiday season.

Serves 6

Baked Tomato Halves

3 medium tomatoes
Salt and pepper
2 tablespoons sugar
1 tablespoon dried basil
1 cup bread crumbs, sautéed in a little butter
3 tablespoons butter

Cut tomatoes crosswise into halves. Place in buttered baking dish, cut side up. Sprinkle halves with salt (use enough), pepper, sugar, and basil. Top with sautéed bread crumbs, pressing them into the tomatoes to absorb juices, then top with a pat of butter. Can be done to this point early in the day; cover and refrigerate.

Preheat oven to 350° and bake tomatoes 10 to 15 minutes, until heated through but not mushy. Put them under the broiler for a few minutes to brown the crumbs, then serve.

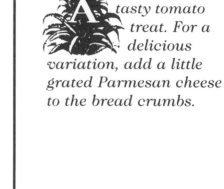

A tasty tomato treat. For a delicious variation, add a little grated Parmesan cheese to the bread crumbs.

Serves 6

Tomatoes Stuffed with Spinach

2½ tablespoons butter
1 clove garlic, peeled and crushed
1¾ pounds spinach, stemmed, well-rinsed, and
    drained
Salt and pepper to taste
Dash of ground nutmeg
3 large tomatoes
3 tablespoons chicken broth or water

Steam the spinach until just wilted. Drain.

Heat the butter in a skillet over medium heat.
Sauté the garlic for 1 minute, then add the
spinach, sprinkle with salt, pepper, and nutmeg,
and sauté for another minute. Remove from heat
and let cool.

Preheat oven to 350°.

Cut the tomatoes in half crosswise and scoop out
the insides (reserve for soup or sauce). Stuff the
shells with the spinach. Pour chicken broth or
water into a small, shallow baking dish or pan,
place tomatoes on it, and bake for 3 to 5 minutes
or until heated through.

Serves 6

A colorful side dish, great for a buffet.

Dilled Cucumbers

3 medium cucumbers
1 tablespoon butter
1 tablespoon fresh minced dill
Salt and pepper to taste

Peel the cucumbers and cut them in half lengthwise. With a teaspoon or melon baller, scoop out all seeds. Cut each piece in half again lengthwise to form 4 long strips and then cut these across (each cucumber yields 8 "sticks").

Heat the butter in a frying pan and sauté cucumbers, covered, until semisoft, about 10 minutes. Add a little hot water and toss them gently to keep from burning. Add salt, pepper, and dill. Toss and sauté 1 minute longer (cucumber should be soft but not limp), and serve.

Especially nice with fish or veal!

Serves 6

Stuffed Acorn Squash

2 small or medium acorn squash
3 tablespoons butter
1 cup chopped onion
1 clove garlic, crushed
½ pound mushrooms, chopped
1 cup tofu, cut in ¼-inch cubes
½ cup grated cheddar cheese
¼ cup blanched and chopped kale
¼ cup chopped walnuts
¼ cup sunflower seeds
¾ cup bread crumbs
3 tablespoons dry white wine
Salt and pepper to taste
2 tablespoons minced parsley

Acorn squash makes an especially attractive container. Cut in half, it's scalloped golden rim displays the filling beautifully. Bake the squash in the morning or early in the day. The stuffing can be done shortly before dinner.

Preheat oven to 350°.

Cut the squash in half through the widest part. On the bottom of one half, cut away the stem to make it level. Scoop out the seeds and place cut side down in a baking dish with 1 inch of water. Bake for 45 to 60 minutes or until tender. Let cool. (This can be done early in the day.)

When ready to serve, sauté the onion in the butter for 15 minutes. Add garlic and sauté 1 or 2 minutes longer. Stir in the mushrooms and sauté for another 5 minutes. Transfer the mix to a bowl and add all other ingredients except the parsley. Mix well and correct the seasoning.

If oven has been off, preheat to 350°.

Lightly sprinkle squash cavities with salt and pepper. Stuff with the filling mixture, dot with butter, and bake, uncovered, for 20 minutes on a greased baking sheet. Sprinkle with parsley and serve.

Serves 2

Stuffed Eggplant with Walnuts and Cheese

1 small eggplant
3 tablespoons olive oil
1 small onion, chopped
2 cloves garlic, crushed
Salt and pepper to taste
1 egg
¼ cup grated Parmesan cheese
2 tablespoons minced parsley
4 tablespoons chopped walnuts
4 tablespoons thick tomato sauce
¼ cup grated Monterey Jack or Swiss cheese

Cut eggplant in half lengthwise. Using a small sharp knife, carefully scoop out each half. Immerse each empty shell in a bowl with cold, salted water. Chop the eggplant pulp coarsely and set aside.

Heat the oil and sauté the onion for 10 minutes. Add the garlic and sauté another minute. Add the eggplant pulp and sprinkle lightly with salt and pepper. Sauté, adding a little water if needed, until eggplant is soft.

In a small bowl, lightly beat the egg with the Parmesan. Stir in the parsley and walnuts. Add to the eggplant, mix well, remove from heat, and cool slightly.

Preheat oven to 350°.

Drain the eggplant shells, fill with the sautéed mixture, dribble the tomato sauce on top, sprinkle with grated fresh cheese, and bake until hot and cheese is bubbly.

Serves 2

This dish is a real treat for lovers of the elegant and under-appreciated eggplant.

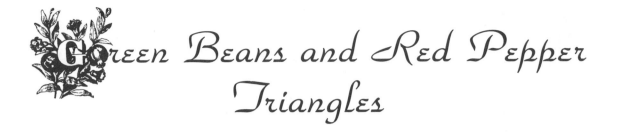

Green Beans and Red Pepper Triangles

1 pound fresh green beans
2 tablespoons butter
Salt and pepper to taste
Half a red pepper

Cut the stems off the beans and plunge them in a large pot of boiling salted water. Boil for 3 to 5 minutes (taste to check on crispy tenderness). Drain beans and immediately immerse in a large container of cold water to stop the cooking and keep the fresh green color. Drain the blanched beans again and refrigerate until ready to use (can be done hours ahead of time).

Cut the red pepper into ½-inch strips and with a sharp knife slice off the inner white membrane. Cut each strip into small triangles and sauté in 1 teaspoon of butter for 1 minute.

In a large frying pan, melt remaining butter. Place the beans in a sieve and immerse in boiling water for a minute to reheat. Drain and add to the butter. Sprinkle with salt and pepper, gently tossing to coat evenly. Place portions on individual serving dishes, top with the red pepper triangles, and serve.

Here's another festive-looking, easy-to-make vegetable dish, delicious in any season.

Serves 6

Glazed Carrots with Snow Peas

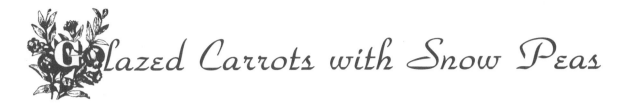

6 medium carrots
1½ tablespoons sugar
1½ tablespoons butter
½ teaspoon salt
1 tablespoon minced parsley
12 snow peas, blanched

Peel the carrots, cut in half crosswise, then quarter each half. Place carrots in a frying pan and add just enough water to barely cover. Add the sugar, butter, and salt. Cover and bring to a boil. Remove the cover and let boil over high heat until the water has evaporated. Carrots will have softened some but should not be limp.

Add the parsley, toss, and remove from heat. Divide carrots into individual servings and garnish each portion with 2 snow peas.

Super-simple, but oh, so tasty!

Serves 6

Zucchini with Peas, Tomatoes, and Walnuts

1 pound small, thin, deep green zucchini
2 tablespoons butter or vegetable oil
1 cup fresh peas (or thawed frozen ones)
¼ pound snow peas, strings removed, blanched
    and cut diagonally in half
4 plum tomatoes, skinned, seeded, and cut into
    thin strips
5 fresh basil leaves, chopped
3 tablespoons chopped walnuts
Salt and pepper to taste

Cut zucchini lengthwise into quarters, then into
½-inch pieces. In a frying pan, heat the butter or
oil and sauté the zucchini for several minutes.
Add peas, toss, and sauté another minute or so,
then add tomatoes, basil, walnuts, salt, and
pepper. Toss and correct the seasoning. Serve
at once.

A wonderful summer side dish for chicken or fish. Looks great next to golden curried rice.

Serves 4 to 6

Zucchini and Garlic Sauté

3 medium zucchini
1 clove garlic, peeled and mashed
3 tablespoons butter
Salt and pepper to taste

Cut the zucchini into ¼-inch slices, then cut each slice into ¼- inch sticks (like tiny French fries). Heat the butter and sauté the garlic for 1 minute. Add the zucchini and seasonings, and sauté for another few minutes until zucchini is heated through but not limp.

Option: For color, add diced red and/or yellow pepper.

Quick and easy and really yummy!

Serves 6

Stuffed Zucchini

1 medium zucchini
2 tablespoons olive oil
2 tablespoons finely chopped onion
1 clove garlic, crushed
2 tablespoons chopped red pepper
2 tablespoons minced parsley
4 to 5 tablespoons Italian bread crumbs
   (or cooked couscous or rice)
¼ cup firm tofu, cut into ¼-inch cubes
Salt and pepper to taste
2 tablespoons tomato sauce
2 teaspoons grated Parmesan cheese

his is a nice variation on a summertime favorite.

Cut the zucchini in half lengthwise. Scoop out the halves with a small spoon or melon baller and chop the pulp. Lightly sprinkle the inside of the shells with salt and set aside.

Heat the oil over medium heat. Add the onion and sauté for 10 minutes. Add the garlic and sauté for another 3 minutes. Stir in zucchini pulp, pepper, and parsley and sauté until almost soft, about 4 minutes. Remove to a small bowl and add bread crumbs and tofu. Mix well, add salt and pepper to taste (undersalt—there'll be more salt in the tomato sauce and Parmesan), and let cool.

Preheat oven to 350°.

Stuff the shells, using all of the mixture. Zucchini will be heaped. Top with tomato sauce, sprinkle with Parmesan, and bake on a small, greased baking pan for 20 minutes.

Serves 2

Red Cabbage in Burgundy Wine

5 tablespoons bacon fat
1 medium onion, diced
4 tablespoons sugar
¼ cup red wine vinegar
¼ cup Burgundy wine
¼ cup water
¼ teaspoon ground cinnamon
1 whole clove
2 pounds red cabbage, finely shredded
Salt and pepper to taste
2 medium-sized tart apples, peeled and shredded
Zest of half a lemon
1 ounce (a jigger) of Burgundy wine
2 tablespoons flour

A hearty, piquant side dish beautifully compatible with robust meats such as beef, pork, or game.

In a large saucepan, heat the bacon fat, add the onions, and simmer for 15 minutes or until soft. Stir in sugar and simmer 5 more minutes. Mix vinegar, ¼ cup wine, and water and stir into the onions. Add the spices and cabbage and enough water to barely cover. Add salt and pepper, bring to a boil, then simmer covered for 1 hour or until almost soft.

Stir in shredded apples and finish cooking, uncovered, until most of the liquid is absorbed and cabbage is soft but not mushy. Add lemon zest and refresh with 1 ounce of Burgundy. Dust with flour to absorb the remaining liquid. Taste and correct the seasoning; there should be a pleasing balance between sweet and sour.

Serves 6

Green Cabbage in Champagne

5 tablespoons butter
1 medium onion, finely chopped
1 teaspoon caraway seeds (optional)
1 tablespoon sugar
¼ cup white wine vinegar
1 cup champagne
1 medium green cabbage, finely shredded and
    rinsed
Salt and pepper to taste
½ cup heavy cream

Melt 3 tablespoons butter in a large saucepan.
Add the onions and sauté for 15 minutes. Add the
caraway seeds and sauté another 5 minutes. Stir
in sugar until dissolved. Add the vinegar and
champagne and stir well. Add cabbage, salt, and
pepper and mix gently to coat with the liquid.
Bring to a boil and cook, uncovered, to reduce
almost all the liquid.

To finish, stir in the heavy cream and
remaining butter. Correct the seasoning with
added salt and pepper if needed, and serve.

An updated version of this traditional Austrian dish, the beloved cabbage. But the cabbage is not cooked to death, and the champagne lends a vivacious delicacy. Great with pork and poultry.

Serves 6

Entrées

Yes, there were mistakes. Like the time I ran late and in my panic grabbed the wrong box and thickened the sauce with baking soda rather than cornstarch. And then there was the time... but never mind; you needn't know everything.

T.C.

Old-Fashioned Roasted Turkey

1 fresh 20-pound turkey
½ cup orange juice
Sprinkling of salt and pepper
Stuffing (see below)
¾ cup softened butter
Paprika

Remove the giblets and set aside. Rinse the turkey inside and out and dry with paper towels. Cut off the wing tips and add them to the giblets. Remove fat and discard. Lightly wet or spray the turkey inside and out with orange juice (a plant mister works beautifully here). Then rub with salt and pepper, again inside and out.

Stuff and truss the turkey. Preheat oven to 325°. Brush turkey all over with melted butter and sprinkle with paprika. Place, breast side up, on rack in roasting pan. Roast for 6 hours, basting every 30 minutes. When breast gets dark, cover it with a piece of cheesecloth or foil. To check for doneness, deeply prick thigh joint with a skewer; liquid should run clear. A thermometer inserted at the same spot would register 180°.

Stuffing

¾ cup butter
4½ cups finely chopped onion
4½ cups finely chopped celery
1¼ cup minced parsley
1½ tablespoons salt
1½ tablespoons poultry seasoning
1½ teaspoons paprika
¾ teaspoon pepper
18 cups diced French or white bread
2 eggs, lightly beaten

In Austria where I grew up, there is, of course, no American Thanksgiving tradition. For the first few years I lived here, I tended to ignore this holiday. We would either go out to dinner or be invited to someone's home. But when our family began to grow and three-year-old Claudia asked if we would have a big turkey like Trisha's. . . . Well, it was time to become American.

But how do I cook such a turkey? Something from scratch, something so different from my recently acquired Chef Boyardee skills? Mildly panicked, I leafed through my Ladies Home Journal *food section, and there it was: a step-by-step plan for the novice cook. It worked so well we have never really deviated from this recipe. I tried fancier versions, but sooner or later I always returned to this honest classic. When the kids grew up and had their own Thanksgiving, they called home for the recipe.*

$\mathcal{M}$elt the butter in a large skillet and sauté the onion and celery for 5 minutes. Transfer to a large bowl and toss lightly with the rest of the ingredients. Set aside (can be done a day ahead of time).

Giblet Gravy

Giblets and wing tips
1 stalk celery, chopped
1 medium carrot, chopped
1 bay leaf
1 medium onion, chopped
½ teaspoon salt
4 peppercorns
½ cup flour
Salt and pepper to taste
1 cup heavy cream

$\mathcal{P}$lace giblets (except liver), celery, carrot, bay leaf, onion, salt, and peppercorns in a saucepan with 6 cups water. Bring to a boil, reduce heat, and simmer, partially covered, for 2¼ hours. Add the liver and simmer 15 minutes more.

$\mathcal{S}$train, setting liquid aside. Remove peppercorns, purée the vegetables in a blender, and save. Dice the meat and save.

$\mathcal{M}$ake the gravy right in the roasting pan. Heat the drippings on the stove. (If there is too much grease in the pan, pour some out and save for other uses.) Stir in the flour, browning it slightly. Remove from heat and whisk in 1 cup cold water to dissolve flour. Return to heat, whisking furiously. When smooth, gradually add enough giblet stock to achieve the consistency you want. Simmer for 10 minutes, whisking often. Add the puréed vegetables and diced meat. Add the cream, correct the taste with salt and pepper, and serve over the carved turkey.

$\mathcal{S}$erves 15 to 20

Stuffed Chicken Breasts with Marsala Sauce

2 large whole skinless, boneless chicken breasts
4 strips bacon
4 slices smoked Gouda cheese
Salt and pepper to taste
½ cup flour
⅓ cup Marsala wine
⅓ cup heavy cream
1 tablespoon minced parsley

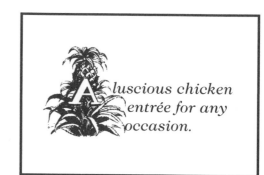

A luscious chicken entrée for any occasion.

Cut the breasts in half and remove tenders (save for another meal), fat, and sinew. With a small, sharp knife carefully cut a pocket in each half.

In a heavy frying pan, lightly brown the bacon (not too crisp; you should be able to bend it). Remove, drain, and cool. Save the pan with the rendered fat.

Stuff each breast with 1 folded slice of bacon and one slice of the cheese. Pin the pocket closed with a toothpick or metal turkey-trussing pin, which is easier to remove later. Lightly sprinkle each breast with salt and pepper and dip in flour.

Quickly brown the chicken breasts on both sides in the hot bacon fat. Remove and keep warm. To the fat, add the wine and cream. Bring to a boil and whisk hard to mix in all the tasty brown pieces in the pan. Reduce heat and return chicken. Cover the pan and simmer the chicken very gently, 5 minutes on each side. Remove the chicken and let cool slightly.

Remove the toothpicks or metal pins (needle-nose pliers will be a great help here). Reduce the sauce to a thick and creamy consistency (if too thick, whisk in a little hot water). Return the chicken to the sauce and turn to coat.

To serve, place one half-breast on each plate, drizzle with sauce, and sprinkle with parsley. Outstanding!

Serves 4

Lemon Chicken

18 chicken tenders (white-meat chicken strips
    often packaged for stir-frying)
Salt and pepper
1 tablespoon fresh lemon juice
2 eggs
2 tablespoons milk
3 cups fresh bread crumbs (8 slices of dry bread
    crumbed in a food processor or blender)
½ cup butter
1 tablespoon fresh lemon juice
½ cup chicken broth
2 tablespoons Curaçao (orange-flavored liqueur)
2 tablespoons minced parsley
6 slices lemon, slashed to center, for garnish

A light entrée, very nice for summer meals.

Between 2 sheets of waxed paper, gently pound the chicken flat. Lay tenders on flat surface, sprinkle lightly with salt and pepper, and rub with a few drops of lemon juice.

In a small bowl, lightly beat the eggs with the milk. Dip chicken into egg mixture and then into crumbs, patting the crumbs firmly into the chicken. (This can be done up to 4 hours ahead; store the chicken on a baking sheet between 2 sheets of waxed paper in the refrigerator.)

When ready to serve, heat the butter in a heavy frying pan and quickly fry the chicken to a golden color, no more than 2 minutes on each side. Remove and drain on paper towels and keep warm.

Reduce heat and add lemon juice, chicken stock and liqueur to the drippings, whisking hard to scrape the brown tasty bits from the pan. Simmer for 15 minutes and correct the seasonings. Sauce should have a pleasant sweet-and-sour citrus taste.

To serve, place 3 slightly overlapping pieces of chicken on each plate, pour some sauce across the center, sprinkle with parsley, garnish with a twisted lemon slice, and serve.

Serves 6

Chicken Roulades with Hollandaise Sauce

1 pound fresh spinach
3 large whole skinless, boneless chicken breasts
Salt and pepper
6 thin slices Virginia baked ham
6 thin slices mozzarella cheese
1 cup flour
3 tablespoons butter
3 tablespoons cooking oil
1 cup hollandaise sauce (next recipe)

Stem and wash the spinach. Steam until just wilted. Drain and cool; squeeze out all excess water by hand and set aside.

Cut the breasts in half and remove all fat and sinew. Carefully pound the breasts (if you pound too hard the chicken may shred) between 2 pieces of waxed paper until almost paper-thin. Chicken should measure roughly 5 x 6 inches and about ⅛ inch thick.

Line up the 6 breast pieces on a flat surface and shape into rectangles. Lightly sprinkle with salt and pepper. Spread each with 1 slice ham, spinach leaves, and 1 slice cheese, stopping ¼ inch from sides and ½ inch from top. Fold in the sides over the stuffing and then roll up each breast, forming the roulade (rolls can be done ahead of time up to this point; cover and refrigerate). When ready to cook, place on a baking sheet, seam side down, and freeze for 15 minutes to help seal the rolls.

These chicken rolls, stuffed with ham, cheese, and bright green spinach, are based on a recipe from Steve Raichlen. As visually delightful as they are tasty, these roulades make a great meal for special guests. They can be made a day in advance. Sensational!

$\mathcal{P}$reheat oven to 400°.

$\mathcal{M}$elt the butter and oil in a heavy frying pan. Dip the chicken roulades in flour and brown them over medium heat, seam side down first. Remove to a baking sheet and place in oven. Bake for 15 minutes. Remove from oven and let rest for 5 minutes before slicing.

$\mathcal{T}$o serve, slice the roulades (an electric knife works best) into ¼-inch slices and place them, overlapping in domino fashion, on top of a hollandaise sauce (tomato sauce is nice, too).

$\mathcal{S}$erves 6

Fluffy Hollandaise Sauce

2 tablespoons fresh lemon juice
3 tablespoons water
1 egg
2 egg yolks
6 ounces unsalted butter
Salt and white pepper
Additional lemon juice to taste
Dash of Tabasco sauce (optional)

Combine lemon juice and water in a small saucepan and heat but do not boil.

In another small saucepan, melt the butter. It should be merely warm, not piping hot.

In a heavy stainless steel or enameled saucepan (avoid aluminum; it gives eggs a greenish cast) vigorously whisk the egg and yolks until light and slightly thick. Place the pan over low heat and continue whisking, gradually adding the lemon juice and water mix. When the eggs begin to thicken to the consistency of mayonnaise, remove the pan from the heat at once – you want a sauce, not scrambled eggs.

Off the heat, and still whisking, add the butter a little at a time until it is completely incorporated. Add salt and pepper and, if necessary, a bit more lemon juice. Serve at once.

Note: If the sauce curdles, add an ice cube and whisk until smooth again. To avoid curdling, place the saucepan on a cake rack on top of a pan of hot (not boiling) water. This way, the sauce will keep for the length of a meal. Leftover hollandaise does not keep and should be discarded.

This is an especially light and "mousse-y" hollandaise, fail-safe, fast, and easy. Wonderful with chicken, fish, asparagus, broccoli, tofu, and, of course, Sunday morning eggs Benedict.

Serves 6

Chicken California

$\mathcal{M}$arinate the chicken the day before serving.

5 whole skinless, boneless chicken breasts
½ cup red wine vinegar
½ cup olive oil
½ cup golden raisins
¾ cup black olives, sliced
½ cup capers
10 cloves garlic, minced
¼ cup oregano
10 pitted prunes or 10 sun-dried tomatoes

½ cup dark brown sugar
1 cup dry white wine
3 tablespoons minced Italian parsley

$\mathcal{T}$rim off any fat from the chicken breasts and cut them in half. Set aside.

$\mathcal{T}$o make the marinade, mix the next 8 ingredients in a deep bowl. Add the chicken and mix well to coat breasts thoroughly. Cover and refrigerate overnight.

$\mathcal{P}$reheat oven to 350°. In a shallow baking pan, arrange breasts in a single layer and top with the marinade. Sprinkle with brown sugar and gently pour the wine around the chicken breasts. Bake uncovered for 25 to 30 minutes or until fork tender, basting once or twice.

$\mathcal{T}$o serve, transfer chicken to plate or platter, top with some of the olives, raisins, capers, and prunes (or tomatoes) and moisten with some of the pan juices. Sprinkle with parsley, and enjoy.

$\mathcal{S}$erves 10

his recipe is in memory of our California years. Like that sunny state's life-style, it lends itself to indoor or outdoor enjoyment. You can serve it hot for dinner, or let it cool (it lasts for days in your refrigerator) and take it to your favorite picnic spot. It's a big hit on our gourmet llama hikes.

Curried Chicken Salad

2 cups chicken stock
¼ cup Tamari soy sauce
1 tablespoon Worcestershire sauce
2 whole skinless, boneless chicken breasts

Curry Mayonnaise

¼ cup good mayonnaise
¼ cup sour cream
2 teaspoons curry powder
¼ teaspoon cayenne
½ teaspoon garlic salt
½ teaspoon Dijon mustard
2 tablespoons chopped mango chutney
1 tablespoon grated orange peel
½ stalk celery, chopped
2 scallions, thinly sliced (tops included)
1 small apple, unpeeled and diced

Garnish

3 tablespoons sliced almonds, toasted
1 scallion, thinly sliced (top included)

A favorite for our buffet brunches, lunches, or dinners!

In a 10-inch frying pan, combine chicken stock, Tamari soy sauce, and Worcestershire sauce. Bring to a boil. Add the chicken, reduce heat, and simmer, covered, until chicken is fork tender (8 to 10 minutes). Remove from heat and let chicken cool in the liquid. Drain and cut into ½-inch chunks.

In a large bowl, combine all ingredients for the curry mayonnaise. Add the chicken and mix well. Cover and chill for several hours or overnight.

Just before serving, sprinkle top with almonds and scallion rings.

Serves 8

Scallops with Mustard Maple Cream Sauce

4 strips bacon, diced
1 teaspoon cooking oil
1 shallot, minced
3 tablespoons maple syrup
1 tablespoon Dijon mustard
4 ounces heavy cream
1 pound scallops
2 tablespoons flour for dusting, or more
  if needed
1 tablespoon cooking oil

Make the base sauce: Sauté the bacon in
1 teaspoon oil until crisp. Add the shallot, sauté
1 minute, then add syrup and mustard. Swirl
and add heavy cream. Mix well and reduce for
2 minutes. Set aside.

Lightly dust the scallops with flour and stir-fry
in an extremely hot pan with 1 tablespoon oil for
1 minute (heat the pan before adding the oil).

Add the base sauce, adjust the taste and
consistency with salt, pepper, and a little extra
cream if needed.

Serves 4

Another wonderful contribution from Perrin Long.

Stuffed Sole Monterey

5 pounds fresh sole filets
Fresh lemon juice
Salt and pepper

Filling

½ pound cooked shrimp, chopped
1 cup steamed and chopped fresh broccoli
1 cup grated Monterey Jack cheese
½ cup crumbled mild blue cheese
3 tablespoons ricotta cheese
⅓ cup sour cream
2 tablespoons minced parsley
½ cup toasted cashews, chopped
Juice of 1 lemon
Salt and pepper to taste
¼ cup dry white wine

Sauce

1 cup dry white wine
1 cup fish stock
1 cup heavy cream
1 tablespoon chopped dill
Salt and pepper to taste
2 tablespoons butter
Dill sprigs for garnish

Spread sole filets on a flat surface and sprinkle with a few drops of lemon juice and just a touch of salt and pepper.

Have you ever been so carried away by a meal that you stormed the kitchen, cornered the chef, and on your knees implored him for the recipe? This just about happened one evening while I was having dinner at the Surfside Resort Inn, a beautiful place on the central Oregon coast. Was it the Pacific sunset? The heady wine? Whatever the reason, I had to go backstage. Randy King, the inn's executive chef, graciously mailed me the recipe, and it's become part of our seafood repertoire. Thanks, Randy!

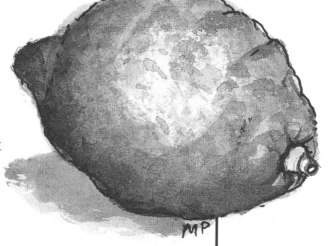

In a bowl, mix all the ingredients for the filling. Correct the taste to your liking. Place 1 tablespoon of mix on each piece of fish, roll up, and set in a pan. Cover and refrigerate for 6 hours.

Preheat oven to 350°. Pour ¼ cup white wine around rolled filets and bake for 30 to 45 minutes.

Make the sauce: In a small saucepan, cook 1 cup of wine until reduced by half. Add the fish stock and reduce by half again. Stir in the cream and again reduce by half. Season with dill, salt, and pepper. Whisk in the butter. Spoon sauce over sole, garnish with dill sprigs, and serve.

Serves 10

Coquilles Saint Jacques

¾ cup dry white wine
2 tablespoons fresh lemon juice
½ teaspoon salt
1½ pounds fresh bay scallops (or sea scallops, cut in half)

¼ cup butter
2 tablespoons green onions
1 clove garlic, crushed
1 cup sliced mushrooms
⅓ cup flour
Dash of white pepper
1 cup milk

1 cup plain bread crumbs
2 tablespoons butter, melted
½ cup grated Parmesan cheese
2 tablespoons minced parsley

Don't be intimidated by the long list of ingredients! This entrée is easy to assemble and will earn you rave reviews.

In a small saucepan, mix wine, lemon juice, and salt. Bring to a boil, reduce heat, and simmer, covered, for 1 minute. Add the scallops and simmer 1 minute longer. Drain, reserving the liquid. (You should have 1 cup; add water if needed.)

In another saucepan, melt the ¼ cup of butter and sauté the green onion and garlic for 1 minute. Add mushrooms and cook until barely tender. Stir in flour and white pepper. Add milk and the reserved cup of scallop cooking liquid. Cook until thick and bubbly. Add a little more salt if needed. Remove from heat and stir in the scallops.

Preheat oven to 400°. Butter 6 coquilles or other oven-proof shallow serving dishes (1 per person) and fill with scallops. Mix the bread crumbs with the melted butter and Parmesan and sprinkle over the scallops. Bake for 10 minutes until lightly browned. Sprinkle with parsley and serve.

Serves 6

Dilled Haddock Parmesan

1 cup sour cream
¼ cup freshly grated Parmesan
¼ cup grated Swiss cheese
1 teaspoon fresh minced dill (or ½ teaspoon
  dried)
¼ cup very soft butter
Salt and pepper to taste

3 pounds haddock filets
Sprinkle of sweet Hungarian paprika
6 sprigs of dill for garnish
6 lemon wedges

In a small bowl, mix the sour cream, cheeses, minced dill, and butter. Add salt and pepper to taste. Set aside.

Preheat oven to 375°.

Cut filets into 6 individual servings and place them on a buttered baking sheet. Top each piece with cheese mixture and bake for 15 to 20 minutes. Sprinkle lightly with paprika, garnish with dill sprig, and serve with a lemon wedge.

I'm very fond of this recipe. It represents one of my first attempts to become a cook. At the time, my partners and I lived in an Exeter condo, waiting to move to Snowvillage Inn. I'd wake up at 2 A.M., scared silly. What had I done, buying an inn that came without a cook? How was I, the Crockpot and pressure-cooker specialist, going to produce gourmet meals for all those guests? I went out and bought a cookbook written by innkeepers. Every day, Frank and Peter bravely served as guinea pigs and judges as I randomly cooked my way through that book. For the first few nights they didn't say much. But when I hit the haddock, they reached for more and said, "It's a winner!" We still serve it, and our guests feel the same way.

Serves 6

Best Beef Bourguignon

¼ cup butter
7½ pounds beef tenderloin tips, cut in 1-inch
    cubes
4½ cups red wine
3 bay leaves
1½ teaspoons thyme
1 teaspoon crumbled rosemary
3½ cups beef broth
4 to 6 tablespoons cornstarch, dissolved in
    ½ cup water
Kitchen Bouquet to taste

2 tablespoons butter
30 firm small mushroom caps
10 thick slices salt pork, diced

2 tablespoons butter
30 frozen pearl onions
3 tablespoons sugar
½ cup beef broth

Melt the butter in a large frying pan and
quickly sear the meat over high heat, about 1
minute on each side. Remove at once and keep
warm. To the pan add the wine, bay leaves,
thyme, and rosemary. Bring to a boil, scraping
loose the brown particles in the pan. Simmer to
reduce by half. Heat the beef broth and add to
the pan; reduce by half again. Add any meat
juices from the seared tenderloin. Transfer
this liquid to a deep pot and thicken with
cornstarch/water mixture. Simmer the sauce
for 10 minutes, whisking often, to eliminate any
starchy taste. Deepen the color to a rich brown
with Kitchen Bouquet.

*We call this the
"best" because
it is made with
tenderloin tips, elevating
the usual stew to a
category of truly festive,
special dishes. And best
of all, it takes far less
time to produce, because
the long hours of
simmering necessary to
tenderize tough meat are
not needed. This recipe is
done in three steps with
three frying pans. Then
everything is combined in
one big pot.*

Melt 2 tablespoons butter in another frying pan. Add the mushroom caps and sauté over medium heat until slightly colored. Remove caps with a slotted spoon and set aside. To the same pan, add the salt pork and sauté until crisply browned. Remove with a slotted spoon and drain on paper towels. Set aside.

In a third frying pan, melt 2 tablespoons butter and sauté the onions over medium heat, sprinkling with 3 tablespoons sugar to glaze until golden. Add ½ cup beef broth to loosen the caramel. Set onions aside.

Add the mushrooms, salt pork, and onions to the sauce. Stir gently, correct the taste with salt and pepper, and 1 to 1½ tablespoons sugar if still too tart. If the bourguignon sauce is still too watery, add more dissolved cornstarch. Just before serving, add the tenderloin and reheat quickly (don't overcook the meat). Sprinkle with parsley and serve. Great with spaetzle, buttered noodles, or mashed potatoes.

Serves 12 to 15

Jaeger Rouladen
(Piquant Stuffed Beef Rolls in Wine Sauce)

Filling

6 slices bacon
1 large onion, minced
2 tablespoons minced parsley
4 tablespoons bread crumbs (pumpernickel
   is best)
6 ounces mushrooms, chopped
6 anchovy filets, chopped
1 tablespoon capers, drained and chopped

Sauté bacon until almost crisp. Remove, cool,
and dice. Set aside. In rendered bacon fat (adding
1 to 2 tablespoons butter if needed), sauté the
onion for 10 minutes. Add parsley, crumbs, and
mushrooms, and sauté 5 minutes more. Remove
from heat, add anchovies, capers, and bacon.
Mix well and let cool.

Rouladen

12 slices bottom-round beef, ¼-inch thick
   (ask your butcher to cut this for you)
2 to 3 tablespoons Dijon mustard
Fresh ground pepper
3 dill pickles, quartered lengthwise
2 cups flour for dredging, or more if needed
4 tablespoons butter
1 cup Burgundy wine
1 cup beef stock

This is an Austrian recipe. Hunter's beef rolls are hearty, savory, man-food for that big appetite. I love this dish, especially in cold weather. But it does take time, so prepare the rolls well in advance. The good news is that they can be made days ahead of time. In fact, they are tastier the longer they marinate. To serve them, simply reheat for 30 minutes in the oven.

Between 2 layers of waxed paper, pound the beef as thin as possible without tearing. Spread slices, narrow side up, on a flat surface, brush with mustard, and sprinkle with pepper. Spread filling on beef, leaving a scant ¼ inch at sides and ½ inch at top. Place 1 strip of pickle across the bottom. Fold sides over filling and roll each slice into a tight, neat roll. Secure the seam with a toothpick. Dredge the rolls in flour, brushing off any excess with your fingers. In a large, heavy frying pan, melt the butter and quickly brown the rolls over high heat, a few at a time to keep from crowding. Remove from pan and keep warm.

Pour excess fat from frying pan. Add wine and beef stock over high heat and whisk hard to loosen tasty brown bits. Reduce heat, place beef rolls back in pan, and simmer, covered, for 1 to 1½ hours. Rolls are done when they almost fall apart when pierced with a fork.

Sauce

½ cup sour cream
Salt to taste
1 tablespoon sugar or Curaçao liqueur
2 tablespoons minced parsley

With a slotted spoon, carefully transfer beef rolls to a covered dish and keep warm. Reduce liquid in pan to about 1½ cups. Whisk in the sour cream and remove from heat. Season to taste with salt, pepper, and sugar or a splash of Curaçao. Sauce should have a robust sweet-and-sour flavor.

To serve, remove toothpicks from rouladen, place 2 on each serving plate, cover with sauce, and sprinkle with parsley.

Great with spaetzle or potato pancakes.

Guten Appetit!

Serves 6

Viennese Beef Tenderloin

Sauce

1 cup orange juice
1 cup Marsala wine
½ cup Burgundy wine
¼ cup brandy
2 cups beef stock
1 cup heavy cream
Pan drippings

Filling

3 strips bacon
2 shallots or ½ red onion, finely
   chopped
2 cloves garlic, mashed
5 ounces mushrooms, chopped
¼ teaspoon fresh minced rosemary
1 teaspoon fresh minced parsley
¼ teaspoon fresh minced marjoram
¼ teaspoon fresh minced thyme
3 tablespoons bread crumbs

Tenderloin

1 whole 5 to 5½-pound beef
   tenderloin, trimmed and
   peeled
Fresh ground pepper
2 teaspoons Dijon mustard
¼ cup butter, softened
6 bay leaves

This is, without doubt, one of our favorite entrées. Wunderbar!

Start with the sauce: In a small saucepan, combine orange juice, wines, and brandy. Simmer to reduce by half. Add the beef stock and reduce by half again. Add the cream, and again reduce by half. Later, add the meat juices from the roasting pan.

Make the filling: Fry, drain, and dice the bacon; set aside. In the same pan, sauté onion for 10 minutes, add garlic, mushrooms, and herbs and sauté briefly. Mushrooms should be soft but not wilted. Remove to a bowl and mix with bacon and crumbs. Let cool.

Preheat oven to 425°.

Now butterfly the tenderloin and lightly pound evenly flat between 2 sheets of waxed paper. Sprinkle with pepper and brush with mustard. Spread the filling, stopping ½ inch from edges. Close the tenderloin and tie with kitchen string in about 6 intervals. Sprinkle with pepper, smear with butter, place bay leaves across top. Place the meat in a well-greased roasting pan and roast for 30 minutes (meat will be medium-rare). Remove and let rest for 5 minutes before carving. Spoon sauce across center of slices and serve.

Serves 10 to 12

Veal Marsala

½ pound mushrooms, sliced
¼ cup butter
4 veal scallopini*
¼ cup Marsala wine
¼ cup chicken stock
1 tablespoon lemon juice
Fresh ground pepper
4 lemon slices
1 tablespoon minced parsley

Melt the butter in a skillet and sauté the mushrooms for about 5 minutes. Remove them with a slotted spoon and set aside in a warm place.

Pound the veal tissue-thin between 2 sheets of waxed paper, being careful not to tear the meat. Lightly dredge the scallopini in flour on 1 side only. Sauté them in the same skillet about 1 minute on each side, floured side first. Remove and keep warm.

Turn up the heat, and into the pan juices whisk the wine, chicken stock, and lemon juice. Reduce briefly. Arrange the veal on individual plates, sprinkle with freshly ground pepper, top with mushrooms, and dribble with sauce. Garnish with parsley and a twisted lemon slice.

*Very thin turkey cutlets may be substituted.

A quick and elegant entrée for spontaneous, intimate dinners. This recipe is less suitable for a large crowd unless you hire somebody to do all the pounding!

Serves 4

Paprikaschnitzel
(Veal Cutlets in Paprika Sauce)

6 4-ounce veal cutlets, halved and pounded*
Salt and fresh ground pepper
Juice of ½ lemon
4 ounces butter
½ cup flour
1 cup dry white wine

4 slabs bacon, diced
2 medium onions, diced
4 teaspoons Hungarian paprika
1 cup chicken stock

¼ cup sour cream
¼ cup heavy cream
1 tablespoon minced parsley

A rich and wonderful Austrian veal dish, one of many culinary discoveries from across the Hungarian border.

Lay pounded cutlets flat and lightly sprinkle with salt and pepper. Rub in a few drops of fresh lemon juice.

Heat butter in a large frying pan. Dredge cutlets in flour, 1 side only, and sauté, floured side first, 1 minute on each side. Remove and keep warm. From the frying pan, drain most of the butter and set aside. Add the wine to the pan, bring to a boil, and scrape up any brown bits. Reduce liquid by half and set aside.

In another pan, sauté the diced bacon. Lift out with slotted spoon and set aside. In the same fat, sauté the onions for 10 minutes or until soft, adding a bit of the saved butter if needed. Add the paprika, sauté for 2 minutes, then add the chicken stock. Simmer for 2 minutes.

Add the onion-paprika mixture to the wine sauce in the first pan. Simmer to reduce by half. Add sour cream, heavy cream, and bacon bits. Reheat but do not boil. Correct the seasoning. Return veal to sauce, cover, and turn off the heat.

To serve, place 2 slightly overlapping pieces of veal on each plate. Spoon some sauce over the veal and sprinkle with parsley.

Serves 6

*Turkey may be substituted.

Veal Piccata

4 boneless veal cutlets, about 5 ounces each*
2 tablespoons butter
2 tablespoons cooking oil
½ cup flour
1 teaspoon fresh lemon juice
¼ cup dry white wine
Fresh ground pepper
2 tablespoons minced parsley
4 slices lemon, slashed to the center

Another savory favorite; a nice light entrée.

Cut each cutlet in half and pound tissue-thin between 2 pieces of waxed paper.

In a heavy frying pan, heat the oil and butter until very hot. Dredge the veal in flour, 1 side only, and place in the hot fat, floured side down. Sauté 1 minute on each side. Remove and keep warm.

For the sauce, whisk the lemon juice and wine into the hot fat and bring to a boil, scraping up all the browned bits. This should only take a minute.

To serve, arrange 2 slightly overlapping pieces of veal on individual plates. Sprinkle with freshly ground pepper, dribble sauce over veal, sprinkle with minced parsley, and garnish with a twisted lemon slice. Serve at once.

Turkey may be substituted.

Serves 4

Wiener Schnitzel

6 fresh veal cutlets*
Salt and pepper
Juice of one lemon
2 cups flour
2 eggs, lightly beaten with 2 tablespoons milk
2 cups plain bread crumbs
1 cup butter
1 cup cooking oil
Lemon wedges and parsley sprigs for garnish

Pound the veal between 2 pieces of waxed paper to ¼-inch thickness. With a sharp knife, make 2 or 3 small incisions around the edge of each cutlet to prevent shrinkage and roll-up during frying.

Lightly sprinkle each cutlet, on 1 side only, with salt and pepper. Rub in a few drops of lemon juice. Dip in flour, lightly patting it into the meat, and shake off the excess. Dip in egg wash, then in bread crumbs. Coat well and shake off excess. The crumbs should cling only lightly to the cutlet.

In a heavy skillet, heat ½ cup butter and ½ cup oil. Test the temperature by dropping a bread crumb into the fat — it should fry immediately. Fry the cutlets until a golden brown, adding butter and oil as needed, about 3 minutes or less on each side. Drain on paper towels and serve at once, garnished with lemon and parsley.

*Turkey may be substituted.

Serves 6

There seems to be nothing more quintessentially Austrian than the famous Wiener Schnitzel. The funny thing is, it used to be Italian. Almost 200 years ago, this delightful and simple veal dish found its way into Vienna, and the Viennese claimed it and made it famous.

A Wiener schnitzel can't be done ahead. Be prepared to fry it at the last minute. If not served fresh from the frying pan, it will lose that wonderful crispness. Better to let your guests wait a bit than to serve something limp and soggy.

Hungarian Gulasch

2 pounds pork tenderloin, trimmed and cut in
  1-inch cubes
Salt and pepper
3 tablespoons bacon fat or butter
2 large onions (12 ounces), chopped
3 cloves garlic, crushed
3 to 4 tablespoons Hungarian paprika
2 tablespoons vinegar
3 tablespoons tomato paste
2 tablespoons caraway seeds
Dash of sugar
Salt and pepper to taste

Lightly sprinkle the pork with a little salt and
pepper. Melt the fat in a frying pan and quickly
brown the meat over high heat. Remove with
a slotted spoon and keep warm.

In the same pan, sauté the onion over low heat
for 15 minutes or until transparent. Add the
garlic and paprika and stir for 1 minute. Add the
vinegar and stir 1 minute more. Stir in tomato
paste, caraway seeds, sugar, and 1 cup water and
simmer until reduced by half. Add salt and
pepper to taste.

Add the pork and all its juices. Heat through
and serve at once with quartered boiled potatoes.

Next to Wiener Schnitzel, the second most popular dish in Austria is Hungarian Gulasch. It is served at lunch, dinner, and even as a late breakfast. Thinned out to soup (Gulaschsuppe), it cures hangovers and restaurants have it on hand New Year's Day and after Carnival parties. It can be made with beef, but my favorite is made with pork tenderloin.

Note: You can use less expensive cuts of pork for Gulasch. Then you sauté the onion first, add the meat and all other ingredients, and simmer (with just enough water to barely cover it) for one hour or until meat is tender.

Serves 6

Pork Dijon

2 pork tenderloins
2 tablespoons butter
½ medium onion, finely chopped
2 tablespoons Dijon mustard
½ cup dry white wine
½ cup heavy cream
1 teaspoon sugar
Salt and pepper to taste
1 tablespoon minced scallions or chives
2 tablespoons finely chopped tomato

Trim the tenderloins and slice diagonally into ½-inch medallions (save ends for a stir-fry). Spread out slices and lightly sprinkle them with salt and pepper on 1 side. Heat butter in heavy skillet and quickly sear the pork medallions. Don't overcook or they will be tough; they should still be raw inside at this point (they'll finish cooking later). Remove from heat and keep warm in a covered dish.

In the same frying pan, sauté the onions over low heat until translucent, adding a little more butter if needed. Stir in the mustard, then add wine, whisking up all brown particles in the pan. After a minute, whisk in the cream and cook over medium heat until slightly thickened. Adjust the taste with sugar, salt, and pepper.

Return pork slices to sauce and simmer over low heat until done, about 5 minutes, turning once. Arrange slices on a warm plate, top with some of the sauce, sprinkle with scallions or chives and tomato. Serve at once.

Serves 4

This is a colorful dish when served with yams and steamed broccoli.

Peter's Famous Real New Mexican Chili

2 pounds lean ground beef

4 long green California peppers, thinly sliced,
  seeds and all

4 jalapeño peppers, thinly sliced, seeds and all
  Important: Peppers must be really fresh, not
  old or canned.

1 large onion, chopped

3 medium tomatoes, chopped

3 29-ounce cans tomato sauce (good quality
  and thick)

Salt to taste

In a frying pan, brown the beef and render all
the fat. Drain the meat and transfer to a large pot.
Add vegetables and tomato sauce and simmer
covered for 3 to 4 hours. Stir every half hour.

Serve with a slice of fresh homemade bread and
a glass of milk.

Serves 10 to 12

We rarely serve lunch. But when we do, it's usually a bowl of Peter's chili offered to starving cross-country skiers just in from the trails. Peter can cook two versions. Depending on the amount of hot peppers, he calls one "real" and one "wimp." I tried the real once and couldn't locate my vocal cords for hours. Happily, the skiers prefer the wimpy kind too, so that's what we (Peter not included) serve. Wimpy or not, the chili has a nice kick to it and warms you wonderfully from the inside out.

Years ago, when Peter worked as a roustabout in the oil patch near Hobbs, New Mexico, he befriended Eddie, whose legal residence was always questionable. After a long summer of tricking and teasing Peter, the greenhorn Yankee, Eddie offered his family's chili recipe as a token of truce. If you're wondering why there are no beans in the recipe, consider Eddie's explanation: "Real chili just has meat. Beans are used as a substitute by those who have no meat – 'Poor Mans Chili.'"

Well, after such a nice parting gift, it's understandable why Peter felt a twinge of remorse about leaving that dead rattlesnake in Eddie's truck. But that didn't stop him from smiling when he heard the scream a mile away. Olé!

Grilled Gingered Lamb Chops

½ cup fresh lemon juice
¼ cup Tamari soy sauce
2 tablespoons Dijon mustard
2 tablespoons honey
3 tablespoons minced fresh ginger
1 clove garlic, crushed
8 lamb chops
Fresh mint leaves
½ cup mint jelly

Combine the first 6 ingredients in a flat baking dish. Add the chops. Marinate them, covered, in the refrigerator for at least 6 hours, turning them once every hour or so.

Grill the chops about 6 minutes on each side, brushing them with the marinade once or twice. Garnish with fresh mint leaves and serve mint jelly on the side.

This is a delicious change of pace from beef, chicken, and seafood entrées.

Serves 4

Lamb Tenderloins with Gingered Hazelnuts

Gingered Hazelnuts

4 tablespoons butter
8 shallots, finely chopped
4 ounces hazelnuts, lightly toasted and chopped
1 teaspoon fresh minced thyme or ½ teaspoon
   dried
3 tablespoons fresh minced crystallized ginger
½ cup fresh minced parsley
Salt and pepper to taste

Melt the butter and sauté the shallots, hazelnuts, and thyme for about 10 minutes until the shallots are translucent. Remove from heat, add ginger, parsley, salt, and pepper. Cool.

Lamb Tenderloins

6 lamb tenderloins
Salt and fresh ground pepper
3 tablespoons butter

Carefully and sparingly trim loins. They are so small that if you cut away too much, nothing will be left! Lightly sprinkle with salt and freshly ground pepper.

Preheat oven to 375°.

Melt butter in a large frying pan and quickly sear loins, about 2 minutes on each side; save pan drippings for sauce. Transfer loins to shallow baking dish and bake for 10 minutes.

This lamb dish takes a little effort, but is worth every minute!

*W*hile meat is baking, prepare the sauce.

Sauce

1 cup Burgundy wine
1 cup beef stock or beef base (can use one boullion cube in a cup of water)
3 tablespoons brandy
3 tablespoons Marsala wine
Pan drippings from seared lamb
2 tablespoons cornstarch dissolved in ¼ cup water (slurry)
1 tablespoon sugar
Salt and pepper to taste

*S*immer the Burgundy wine in a small pot until reduced by half. Add the beef stock, brandy, and Marsala and reduce by half again. Add the pan drippings. Thicken slightly with cornstarch slurry, whisking and simmering for 3 minutes until starchy taste has cooked away. Adjust the taste with sugar, salt, and pepper.

*W*hen lamb is cooked, remove to cutting board and slice diagonally. To serve, place lamb slices on top of sauce and sprinkle with the gingered hazelnuts.

*S*erves 6

Potatoes, Rice and Pasta

From experience, I know that recipes, more often than not, are reshaped by the kinds of accidents, emergencies, and whims that spur your creativity into high gear. And that's good. It keeps the fun alive and the joy flowing to your hands and into the food.

T.C.

Parsley Potatoes

12 small or 6 medium potatoes
1 quart chicken broth or salted water
4 tablespoons butter
¼ cup fresh minced parsley

Peel the potatoes. If you use medium potatoes, quarter them. Boil potatoes in chicken broth or salted water until tender but not mushy. Drain and quickly sauté in melted butter. Toss with parsley and serve.

An Austrian staple that goes with anything!

Serves 6

 Potatoes Fritz

2 tablespoons butter
1 small onion, finely chopped
12 small red potatoes
1 to 2 cups chicken stock
3 tablespoons grated Parmesan cheese

Melt the butter in a small frying pan and sauté the onion until soft, about 15 minutes. Remove from heat and set aside.

Scrub and slice the potatoes in such a way that the potato keeps its original shape (imagine a boiled egg sliced with an egg cutter). Slices should be less than ¼ inch thick. Place the sliced potatoes in a small, square, ungreased casserole, separating the slices a bit so they overlap. Barely cover potatoes with chicken stock.

Preheat oven to 350°.

Sprinkle onions and Parmesan across center of potatoes and bake, uncovered, for 20 minutes or until done. Liquid should be mostly absorbed.

Serve each person 2 potatoes (about 8 or 10 slices), fanned out in an attractive curve on one side of the plate.

Serves 6

A young chef who visited here when the inn was closed cooked this for Peter, Frank, and me. "Why is this called Potatoes Fritz?" I asked, always curious about the history of a new dish. "Who is Fritz?" The young chef didn't know and I still don't know. All I know is, Fritz had a way with potatoes. We could have changed the name. But I began to imagine Fritz in all his Teutonic charm (blond, blue-eyed, and dimpled), cruising about his kitchen, fooling around with a German's favorite vegetable. Potatoes Fritz. Has a nice ring to it. I can't think of a better name, actually.

Roasted Red Potatoes

9 small red potatoes
Vegetable oil
Salt to taste
1 tablespoon minced parsley or mint

Preheat oven to 400°. Brush a baking sheet with oil.

Scrub the potatoes and cut them in half crosswise. Lightly sprinkle the cut sides with salt and place the potato halves, cut side down, on the baking sheet. Sparingly brush the tops with oil and sprinkle very lightly with salt.

Bake for 15 to 20 minutes or until soft. Lift potatoes with a metal spatula. Serve 3 potato halves, cut side up, sprinked with parsley or mint, per person.

These dark, unpeeled little potatoes, showing off their golden-brown cross sections, are a simple and lovely contrast to fish and most unsauced meats.

Serves 6

Twice Baked Potatoes

10 medium russet potatoes
Cooking oil
6 ounces cream cheese, softened
1 cup sour cream or plain yogurt
¼ cup toasted onion flakes
1 teaspoon garlic powder
¾ teaspoon white pepper
2 tablespoons butter
½ cup grated Parmesan cheese
Salt to taste
Paprika for garnish

Preheat the oven to 350°. Scrub the potatoes, then rub with oil and place them on an oiled baking sheet. Pierce each potato with a fork 2 or 3 times. Bake the potatoes for 1 hour or until soft.

Remove from the oven and let cool for 5 minutes. With a sharp knife, slice off the tops and scoop out the potato pulp. In a large bowl, combine the potato pulp, cream cheese, sour cream or yogurt, onion flakes, garlic powder, white pepper, butter, and grated cheese. Mash and mix well. Taste and adjust the seasoning with salt.

Fill the potato shells with this mixture, making high mounds (they'll shrink); sprinkle with paprika. You can do the potatoes hours ahead of time to this point.

Preheat oven to 350° (if it's been off). Make sure potatoes are room temperature before baking. Bake 15 to 20 minutes, until nice and hot. Serve at once.

Serves 10

Looking through old kitchen files shortly after we bought the inn, I came across a hand-written recipe called "Do Ahead Party Mashed Potatoes." Supposedly you can keep the unbaked mix in the fridge for two weeks. I've never tried that, but since I needed a good substantial accompaniment for the beef tenderloin and baked potatoes are so much easier to serve to a crowd, I experimented. The twice baked potato became an instant hit. I didn't know where the recipe had come from, but when I served it to Ralph MacLean, one of our most loyal guests, he recognized it as his!

Platzki

(Raw Potato Pancakes)

3 medium potatoes, peeled
1 egg
2 rounded tablespoons flour
Salt and pepper to taste
Oil for frying

Finely grate 2½ of the potatoes, using a hand grater or food processor. Coarsely grate (for crunch) the remaining half. Mix all potatoes together. Add the egg, flour, and seasonings. Work quickly to prevent potatoes from darkening.

Generously cover the bottom of a large frying pan with oil. Bring the oil to a high heat. Drop the potato mix into the hot oil, 1 heaping tablespoon at a time; flatten with a spoon. Quickly fry to a golden brown, turn, and fry the other side.

Lift the pancakes out and drain on paper towels for just a minute. Serve at once, as pancakes lose their crispness if kept waiting.

Serves 10

This is a dish from my childhood. Great with pork, of course, but also delicious with poultry, game, or lamb. Potato pancakes are wonderful served with applesauce, sour cream, or yogurt.

Sweet Potatoes with Orange Juice

6 cups peeled and diced sweet potatoes
4 tablespoons butter
½ cup orange juice
Salt to taste
3 tablespoons toasted sliced almonds

Put the potatoes in a saucepan and barely cover with water. Bring to a boil and cook until very tender. Drain and mash with butter. Add the orange juice. (You can also purée them in a food processor.) Add salt to taste.

Serve, sprinkled with the toasted almonds (or walnuts or pecans).

I learned this recipe from Charlene Thurston, our long-time breakfast cook, who also pitches in at dinner now and then. The orange juice, instead of the usual milk, makes a wonderful difference. We often serve the sweet potato with its rich tangerine color alongside tomato-garnished pork Dijon and emerald broccoli—a feast for the eyes as well as the palate!

Serves 6

Orzo Parmesan

1 pound orzo
4 quarts boiling salted water
2 tablespoons cooking oil
1 cup freshly grated Parmesan
2 tablespoons chopped fresh herbs (parsley, basil, oregano – one or a combination)

Cook the orzo according to directions on the box. Drain and place in a large bowl. Mix with oil until orzo is well coated. Add Parmesan and herb(s), mix well, and serve.

Can be done ahead of time and reheated, covered, in the oven.

Very fast and easy!

Serves 8 to 10

Spaetzle

Salt
2 tablespoons cooking oil

¾ cup milk
3 eggs
2 cups flour
Salt and pepper to taste
4 tablespoons butter
3 tablespoons grated Swiss cheese
1 tablespoon fresh minced parsley

*H*eat a large pot of water to a boil. Add some salt and 2 tablespoons oil.

*B*eat the eggs into the milk. In another bowl, combine the flour with salt and pepper. Add the milk and egg mixture and mix well. Add more salt if needed. Check the texture: dough should drop from a lifted spoon (a bit firmer than applesauce).

*P*lacing the grater across the pot of boiling water, pour enough dough to fill the box on the grater. Move the box back and forth slowly; spaetzle will fall into the water in small drops. When they float to the top, let them cook gently for 5 minutes. Remove with a slotted spoon. Repeat the process until all the dough is used.

*H*eat the butter in a frying pan and sauté spaetzle over medium heat for several minutes. Mix with cheese, sprinkle with parsley, and serve.

A popular Austrian pasta, especially good with hearty, savory sauces. You will need a spaetzle grater, an inexpensive, handy tool available in most good kitchen supply or gourmet stores.

*S*erves 6

Green Rice Angelo

3 cups cooked rice
1 pound sharp cheese, grated
10 ounces chopped spinach, cooked and drained
¼ cup butter
1 cup milk, heated
4 eggs
1 tablespoon minced onion
1 tablespoon Worcestershire sauce
½ teaspoon thyme
1½ teaspoons salt
Pinch of rosemary and marjoram

Combine rice, cheese, and spinach. Melt the butter in the milk and add this to the rice mixture. Slowly add the eggs, 1 at a time. Add the seasonings and mix well.

Preheat oven to 350°.

Pour the rice mixture into a buttered 5-quart casserole. Place the casserole in a pan of hot water, which should come halfway up the sides of the casserole. Bake for 45 minutes. Let set 10 to 15 minutes before serving.

Great with lamb or beef.

Serves 6

Holiday Rice

(White and Wild Rice with Almonds and Raisins)

1 cup white rice
1 cup wild rice
4 cups chicken stock, boiling
2 tablespoons butter
1 cup golden raisins
½ cup dry sherry
1 cup slivered almonds
4 tablespoons butter
2 stalks celery, diced
¼ cup sliced green onions (with tops)
¼ cup fresh minced parsley

We often use this festive rice dish at special functions (weddings, celebrations, holiday buffets). It tastes wonderful, looks great, and can be made in advance. Terrific with chicken or lamb.

Place the white rice in one pot, the wild rice in another. To each, add 2 cups chicken stock and 1 tablespoon butter. Bring to a boil, cover, reduce heat to a simmer, and cook until rice is tender: the white rice 15 to 20 minutes, the wild about 40 to 50 minutes. Decant both the wild and white rice into a large bowl and mix gently.

Put raisins and sherry into a small pot, heat to boiling, and set aside to cool so the raisins will soak up the sherry.

Melt 2 tablespoons butter in a small frying pan and lightly toast the almonds, stirring often. Remove from heat and let cool.

Melt the rest of the butter in another small frying pan and sauté the celery until just soft, about 5 minutes. Add the green onions and parsley and toss together. Remove from heat. Combine raisins, almonds, celery, onions, and parsley with the rice. Correct the taste with salt and freshly ground pepper.

Note: You can use other nuts such as walnuts or pecans instead of almonds, and can add mushrooms, various fresh herbs, sliced black olives, diced ham — you name it.

Serves 10

Parmesan Risotto

5 cups chicken stock, or more if needed
2 tablespoons cooking oil
½ cup diced onion
2 cups white rice (preferably arborio)
¾ cup dry white wine
1 tablespoon butter
¾ cup freshly grated Parmesan cheese
2 tablespoons fresh minced parsley

In a saucepan, bring the chicken stock to a steady simmer.

Heat the oil in a casserole. Add the onion and sauté for 2 to 3 minutes until soft but not brown. Add the rice and stir to coat. Stir in the wine, ¼ cup at a time, and cook until the rice has completely absorbed the wine.

Start adding the simmering broth, ½ cup at a time, adding more only after it has been almost completely absorbed. Keep adding broth in stages for 18 to 20 minutes, until rice is tender but still firm.

Add the butter, Parmesan, and parsley. Mix well and serve warm.

Serves 10

Rice the Italian way – rich, satisfying, and tasty, a welcome change from the usual bland fare. Served with a salad, it can be a meal in itself, but this rice is also a great companion to boiled, broiled, or grilled meat, seafood, and poultry.

Rice Pilaf with Pepper Confetti

1½ tablespoons butter
½ cup finely chopped onion
1 cup white rice
2 cups chicken stock

1½ tablespoons butter
1 clove garlic, crushed
½ red pepper, finely chopped
½ yellow pepper, finely chopped
½ green pepper, finely chopped
Salt and pepper to taste

Melt 1½ tablespoons butter in a small saucepan and sauté the onion for 15 minutes or until soft. Add the rice, mix well, and cook for another 2 minutes, stirring often. Rice should look shiny and translucent. Add the chicken stock and bring to a boil. Cover the pan tightly and reduce heat. Simmer rice 15 to 20 minutes, without stirring, until cooked but firm, and all the liquid is absorbed.

Melt 1½ tablespoons butter in a larger frying pan and sauté the garlic and peppers until soft but still somewhat crispy, about 10 minutes or less. Mix the rice with the vegetables and serve.

Serves 6

A colorful and very tasty way to serve rice.

Desserts

This cookbook represents favorites of our guests.
They are tried and proven recipes, fail-safe
if you follow them closely. Still, you may decide
to treat them as the living, organic things
they really are, and use them as building blocks
for your own creations. Whatever you do,
I wish you much fun and success.

T.C.

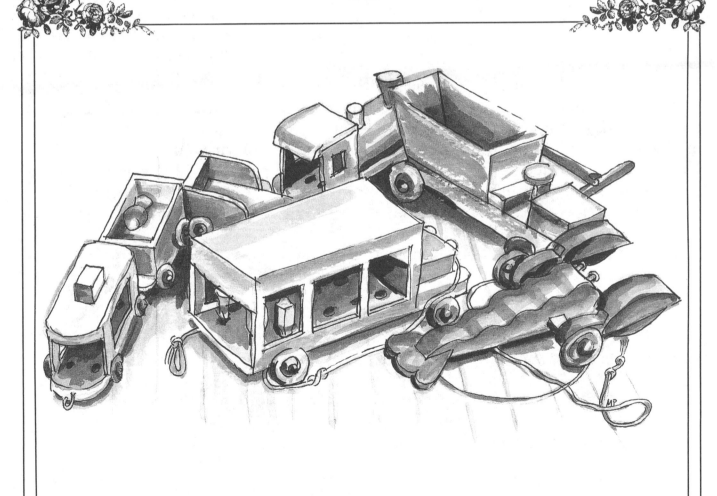

Pears Malakoff

2 cups dry red wine
1 cup crème de cassis
2 cinnamon sticks
6 whole cloves
Zest of one lemon
½ to 1 cup sugar (to taste)
6 ripe Anjou or bosc pears with stems if possible
¼ cup slivered or sliced almonds
6 plain ladyfingers
3 tablespoons amaretto
3 tablespoons unsalted butter, melted
1 16-ounce can pitted bing cherries
1 cup heavy cream, whipped and slightly
    sweetened
6 fresh mint leaves

Pears poached in spiced wine syrup, stuffed with amaretto-soaked ladyfingers, and served with cherry sauce and whipped cream. . . . Sometimes I pick two recipes, take a little from each, and create something new. This is a hybrid of Steven Raichlen's Poached Pears and my mother's all-time favorite dessert, the Malakoff Torte.

In a wide saucepan, combine the wine, crème de cassis, spices, lemon zest, and sugar. Bring to a boil, then simmer for 10 minutes. Peel the pears, then core them from the bottom, leaving stems in place. Put them in a bowl of water to keep from discoloring. When all pears are ready, drain and place upright in the wine. Poach the pears for 12 minutes (or more if necessary). They should be soft but not mushy. Let them cool in the liquid. The pears can be stored that way in the refrigerator 3 or 4 days ahead of serving time.

In a food processor grind the almonds to a coarse meal. Add ladyfingers, amaretto, and butter; process briefly. Stuff the pears with this mixture.

Drain the cherries, reserving 6 for garnish, and cook their liquid, reducing it to about ⅓ cup. Purée cherries in the food processor, then press through a fine strainer. Mix the reduced liquid with the purée.

To serve, spoon the cherry sauce onto 6 plates and set a pear in the center of each. Next to the pear, pipe (with a pastry bag) or spoon a dollop of sweetened whipped cream, garnished with a cherry and mint leaf.

Serves 6

Fresh Fruit Cup with Minted Ginger Sauce

Sauce

1 cup orange juice
⅓ cup sugar
1 tablespoon fresh lemon juice
3 tablespoons rum
1 tablespoon minced fresh or crystallized ginger
1 tablespoon minced fresh mint

In a small saucepan, mix the orange juice, sugar, and lemon juice. Bring to a boil. Lower heat and simmer, uncovered, for 20 minutes. Stir occasionally. Remove from heat and let cool for 10 minutes. Stir in rum, ginger, and mint. Set aside. Prepare the fruit.

Fruit

1 small pineapple
½ pound seedless green grapes
1 pint fresh strawberries
2 tablespoons sugar

Peel, quarter, and core the pineapple. Cut each quarter in half lengthwise. Cut that into very thin, fan-shaped slices and place them in a bowl. Rinse the grapes and cut them in half lengthwise. Add them to the pineapple. Pour the sauce over the fruit, cover, and chill. Rinse, hull and halve the strawberries. Place them in a separate bowl and gently mix them with the sugar. Chill.

Shortly before serving, add the strawberries to the pineapple and grapes (if done far in advance, strawberries will lose their color). Mix gently and serve. Especially attractive if served in broad champagne glasses with a sprig of mint on top.

Serves 6

This light dessert, a welcome change from the usual pies and mousses, is especially appropriate after a substantial entrée such as beef, pork, or richly sauced seafood. It's also great for picnics and summer buffets.

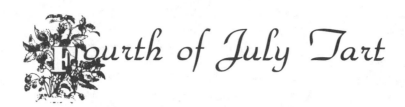

Fourth of July Tart

Pastry Shell

1 cup flour
2 tablespoons sugar
¼ teaspoon salt
4 ounces butter, chilled and cut into small pieces
1 large egg, beaten lightly

Place the flour, sugar, and salt in the bowl of a food processor. Spin 2 seconds just to mix. Then add the butter and process for no more than 30 seconds. Mixture should resemble coarse meal. Add the egg and process in spurts for 1 or 2 minutes, just until the dough comes together into a ball, no longer. Remove dough, wrap, and chill for at least 30 minutes.

Turn the dough out onto a lightly floured board. Flour the ball, flatten lightly with a rolling pin, and roll into a 12-inch round, turning often to keep from sticking. Line a 10-inch tart pan (one with fluted sides and a removable bottom), pressing the sides into place. Trim excess dough with scissors, leaving a ½-inch overlap. Fold this inside to form a double-thickness rim which should extend about ¼ inch above the pan. Place pastry shell on a baking sheet and chill for 10 minutes in the freezer.

Preheat oven to 375°.

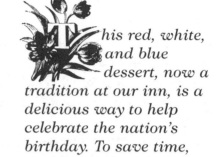

This red, white, and blue dessert, now a tradition at our inn, is a delicious way to help celebrate the nation's birthday. To save time, the pastry shell can be made days in advance and frozen.

To "blind-bake" the crust, line it with aluminum foil, pressing it firmly into the corners. Fill the lined crust with dried beans to keep the shell in place. Bake for 30 minutes. Remove from the oven and carefully lift out the foil with the beans. Return the shell to the oven and bake for about 10 minutes more. If shell puffs up during that time, prick it with a fork. When done, shell should be thoroughly dry and lightly browned (if rim gets done too fast, protect it with a strip of foil). Remove pastry from oven and let cool completely.

Filling

½ cup apricot jam
1 pint fresh strawberries, rinsed, hulled, and halved
2 bananas, sliced crosswise and dipped in lemon or orange juice to prevent browning
1 cup fresh blueberries
⅓ cup sugar
1 envelope unflavored gelatin
3 tablespoons sugar

Heat the apricot jam and whisk until soft and smooth. Brush the bottom of the pastry shell with jam. Starting along the side of the shell, arrange the strawberries, cut side down, in a large circle. They should overlap each other ("piggyback") so their tops are even with the top of the pastry. Inside the circle of strawberries, form a ring of banana slices in the same way, then make a large inner circle of blueberries. A few smaller strawberries might fit in the center. Have fun and be creative! Sprinkle ⅓ cup sugar over berries and bananas.

In a small pot, sprinkle the gelatin over 1 cup cold water. Let stand 1 minute, then stir over low heat until dissolved. Add 3 tablespoons sugar and bring to a boil. Remove from heat and let cool. When just beginning to gel, slowly pour or spoon the gelatin over the berries and bananas; this will hold everything in place. Chill the tart for at least 4 hours.

Serve plain or with a dollop of whipped cream or sweetened yogurt.

Serves 8

Frozen Chocolate Mousse

12 ounces semisweet chocolate, broken into
　　pieces
⅔ cup water
1 cup sugar
¼ teaspoon salt
4 eggs, separated
2 teaspoons vanilla
4 cups heavy cream

In a small double boiler, combine chocolate
with water. Heat to melt. Add the sugar and salt
and whisk until sugar dissolves.

In a bowl, beat the yolks slightly, just to break
and mix. Slowly beat in the chocolate and vanilla.
Set aside and let cool.

Meanwhile, beat the egg whites until fluffy.
Gradually add the sugar and beat vigorously until
stiff. Whip the cream.

Carefully fold the meringue and cream into the
chocolate. Transfer to an 8- or 9-inch springform
pan and freeze for at least 6 hours (best done a
day ahead of serving time).

Optional garnish might be a puff of whipped
cream centered with a fresh raspberry . . . or a
quartet of chocolate chips . . . or a mint leaf or. . . .

*This is a great
backup dessert.
You can take
what you need and keep
the rest, well wrapped in
plastic wrap and foil, in
the freezer.*

　　*After a rich entrée, we
might serve just a narrow
wedge, laid on its side,
thus doubling the yield.*

16 rich servings

Pie Crust

2 cups flour
½ teaspoon salt
2 teaspoons sugar (for sweet fruit pies only)
8 tablespoons butter, chilled, cut into pieces
4 tablespoons vegetable shortening, chilled
5 to 7 tablespoons ice water

This is a basic 9-inch double-crust recipe. If you need a single crust only, just divide the recipe in half.

Mix the flour, salt, and sugar in a mixing bowl. Cut in the butter and shortening, using a knife or pastry blender. Blend quickly until mixture resembles coarse crumbs.

Mix in the ice water, a little at a time and just enough for the dough to come together. Transfer dough to a lightly floured surface and knead briefly until blended and smooth. Gather into a ball, divide in half, shape each half into a ball, flatten slightly, and wrap in plastic wrap or waxed paper. Refrigerate both halves for at least 30 minutes.

Using one half at a time, roll dough out on slightly floured surface to desired size, line the pie pan, and follow the rest of your pie recipe.

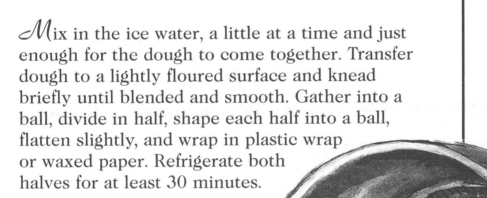

Makes double crust

Crème de Menthe Pie

1½ cup finely crushed chocolate chip cookie
    crumbs
¼ cup butter, melted
24 large marshmallows
⅔ cup milk
1 cup heavy cream
3½ ounces crème de menthe

For the crust, preheat oven to 350°.

Reserve ¼ cup of the cookie crumbs to
sprinkle on top of finished pie. Mix remainder
with melted butter and press onto bottom of an
8-inch pie pan. Bake the crust for 10 minutes
and let cool.

For the filling, heat marshmallows in a double
boiler with the milk. Stir smooth, remove from
heat, and cool. Stir occasionally to avoid
separating.

Whip the cream until stiff. Gently add crème de
menthe to the whipped cream, and carefully fold
this mixture into the cooled marshmallows. Pour
into crust. Sprinkle with reserved cookie crumbs
and chill for at least 3 hours.

Garnish each piece with a dollop of sweetened
whipped cream topped with a fresh mint leaf, a
fanned-out strawberry, or several chocolate chips
arranged in a pattern.

Back in the 1960s when we lived in Columbus, Indiana, then a town of 28,000 people, I discovered this recipe in the local newspaper. The pie was the Grand Prize Winner at the local 4-H Fair. Because it involved minimal baking and because I like crème de menthe, I at once tested it on my young family. Everyone loved it, but Peter especially enjoyed it. It was (and still is) his all-time-favorite dessert. No more traditional birthday cakes for him after that; it had to be a crème de menthe pie — usually one for the family and one for himself (yes, he ate the whole thing). And now we serve it at the inn.

I never met the author of this recipe, but I'm sure she'd smile if she knew what she had started.

Serves 8

# Maple Rhubarb Pie

⅔ cup sugar
2 tablespoons flour
Dash of salt
2 egg yolks
2 teaspoons water
2 cups diced rhubarb
1 unbaked 9-inch pie shell
A small pitcher of real maple syrup

Preheat oven to 400°.

Mix the sugar, flour, and salt. Add the egg yolks and water and mix well. Add the rhubarb and stir until well coated. Turn mixture into the unbaked pie shell and bake for 20 minutes. Reduce heat to 350° and bake exactly 20 minutes more. Cool on a rack.

To serve, pour maple syrup across each wedge.

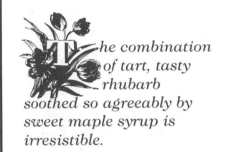

The combination of tart, tasty rhubarb soothed so agreeably by sweet maple syrup is irresistible.

Serves 8

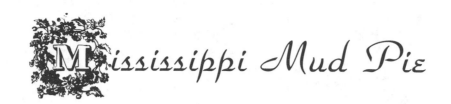

Mississippi Mud Pie

Crust
1½ cups chocolate wafer crumbs
¼ cup butter, melted

Filling
1 quart coffee ice cream
1 pint chocolate ice cream
3 tablespoons coffee-flavored liqueur

Sauce
4 ounces unsweetened chocolate, broken into
    small pieces
1 cup milk or half-and-half
½ cup sugar
⅓ cup light corn syrup
3 tablespoons butter
1 tablespoon vanilla

Garnish
Sweetened whipped cream
Grated chocolate, or a handful of chocolate chips

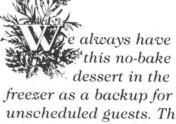

We always have this no-bake dessert in the freezer as a backup for unscheduled guests. The contrast of ice cream flooded with a warm chocolate sauce lends special interest to this otherwise simple pie. Many guests have asked us for this recipe, and some have called to make sure we'd serve it the next time they came!

For the crust, thoroughly blend crumbs and butter. Firmly press onto bottom and sides of a 9-inch pie pan. Freeze until firm.

For the filling, place ice creams in a large bowl. Let soften at room temperature for about 15 minutes. Blend and mix with the coffee liqueur. Turn into frozen crust. Smooth the top and freeze until firm.

Make the sauce: Combine chocolate pieces, milk or half-and-half, sugar, and corn syrup in a medium saucepan. Cook over low heat until chocolate is melted, stirring constantly. Remove from heat. Stir in butter and vanilla. Pour into a serving pitcher and keep warm (or reheat in the microwave).

Cut pie into 8 to 10 pieces. Garnish each piece with a dollop of whipped cream, sprinkle with grated chocolate or a few chocolate chips. Serve in a puddle of warm sauce – incredible!

Serves 8 to 10

French Silk Pie

3 egg whites, room temperature
Pinch of salt
¼ teaspoon cream of tartar
½ teaspoon vanilla
¾ cups sugar
⅓ cup finely chopped walnuts

2 ounces unsweetened chocolate
1 cup butter, room temperature
4 eggs
1½ cups sugar
2 teaspoons vanilla

1 cup heavy cream
1 tablespoon crème de cacao
Semisweet chocolate shavings for garnish

A rich, luxurious chocolate filling, resting on airy meringue and topped with clouds of whipped cream, this is our favorite Saturday night dessert. So you jog that extra mile; it's worth it!

This recipe came with the inn. Charlene Thurston (who also came with the inn, much to our relief) bakes all our breads, most of the desserts, and those incredible chocolate chip cookies. She doesn't remember exactly where this recipe for silk pie came from, but she sure has a magic touch with it!

Note: Bake at least 5 hours before serving.

Preheat oven to 275°. Beat egg whites with salt, cream of tartar, and vanilla until just fluffy, then gradually add the sugar. Beat until meringue is light and firm. Spread into an ungreased 9-inch pie pan. Using a small rubber spatula, build a free-form rim of meringue at least ½ inch higher than rim of pie pan; it should resemble a mountain panorama, with some peaks here and there. Sprinkle rim and bottom with walnuts. Bake meringue for 1 hour, then turn off heat but leave meringue in the oven to cool and dry.

Make the filling. Melt 2 ounces chocolate in a small double boiler. Briefly beat the softened butter in the food processor. Add the eggs, sugar, vanilla, and melted chocolate and process for 15 *minutes* (color will change from a light to a dark brown). Empty filling into a bowl, cover, and chill for at least 4 hours to set.

An hour before serving, fill the meringue shell with the now firm chocolate cream. Whip the heavy cream with the crème de cacao and spread over the pie. Sprinkle with chocolate shavings and serve.

Serves 8

Real New England Apple Pie

Pie Crust

2 cups flour, mixed with a dash of salt
⅓ pound lard, chilled
⅓ cup ice water

In a large bowl, cut the lard into the salted flour, using a knife or a pastry cutter. Add the ice water and mix in with a fork. Remove dough to a pastry board and quickly knead for 2 minutes or until it looks smooth and holds together. Divide in half and roll out each half no more than ¼-inch thick. Use one to line a 9-inch pie pan; keep lined pan and top crust chilled.

Filling

6 to 8 large Granny Smith apples
½ cup sugar
¼ cup Minute Tapioca
⅓ teaspoon ground cinnamon
3 tablespoons butter, cut in small bits
2 tablespoons milk, or more if needed

Preheat the oven to 350°.

Peel and core the apples and slice them about ¼-inch thick. Place them in a large bowl and toss well with the sugar, tapioca, and cinnamon. Fill the pie shell with the apples, mounding lightly in the center, and dot with a bit of extra butter. Cover with the top crust. Wet your fingers to seal the crust together and crimp the edges. With a sharp knife, cut several vents in the top crust. Brush it with milk and bake for 1 hour.

Let cool but don't chill; it tastes best at room temperature. Serve plain or with vanilla ice cream. *Wicked good!*

Serves 8

This is how Charlene bakes apple pie. She is a true native, born and raised right here in our neighborhood, and her pie is a regional classic. Lucky for us and our guests!

Trudy's Viennese Apple Cake

1 tablespoon butter, or more if needed
¼ cup plain white bread crumbs, or more if
  needed
7 ounces (1¾ stick) unsalted butter, room
  temperature
3 eggs, separated
1 cup sugar
2 cups flour
1 tablespoon baking powder
6 to 7 tablespoons heavy cream

4 medium-sized Granny Smith or other tart apples
2 to 3 tablespoons sugar
¼ teaspoon ground cinnamon
Zest of 1 lemon
½ cup sliced almonds
Powdered sugar

An exceptionally fine coffee cake my mother used to bake whenever she visited us.

Thoroughly butter the bottom and sides of a 10-inch springform pan and coat with bread crumbs. Set aside.

Beat the butter until very fluffy, then add the egg yolks and sugar. Mix the flour with the baking powder and add to the butter-egg mixture. Dough should be quite stiff, but if it is too unwieldy, add enough heavy cream to make it manageable.

Beat the egg whites with a dash of salt until stiff and firm. Peel and thinly slice the apples and mix them with the sugar, cinnamon, and lemon zest.

Preheat oven to 350°.

Carefully fold the beaten egg whites into the dough. Using a rubber spatula, carefully spread half the dough onto the bottom of the springform pan (dip the spatula into hot water now and then to facilitate spreading). Scatter apples on top, then cover them as much as possible with the other half of the dough. Sprinkle with almonds and bake for 1 hour. Check with a toothpick for doneness.

Dust heavily with powdered sugar while cake is still hot. Let cool, but don't chill, and serve.

Serves 8

Easy Viennese Apple Strudel

7 medium-sized apples
Dash of rum
¾ cup sugar
1 tablespoon ground cinnamon
Zest and juice of 1 lemon
1 8-ounce package phyllo pastry sheets, 9 x 13
   inches
¼ pound unsalted butter, melted, or more
   if needed
1 scant cup of plain white bread crumbs
1 scant cup golden raisins
½ cup chopped walnuts
Powdered sugar for garnish
1 cup whipped cream, slightly sweetened and
   laced with a dash of rum

Preheat the oven to 350°.

Peel, core, and thinly slice the apples. Mix them with a dash of rum, sugar, cinnamon, lemon zest, and juice. Set aside.

Place a clean cloth, slightly larger than the phyllo sheets, on your counter (a piece of old sheet or kitchen towel will do). Place 1 pastry sheet, wider side facing you, on it. Using a pastry brush, gently brush sheet with the melted butter. Cover with another sheet and brush again. Repeat until there are 8 sheets, brushing each with butter before adding the next (it helps to keep the unused pastry sheets covered with a lightweight, damp cloth to keep them from drying out). Again, brush the top of the eighth sheet with butter.

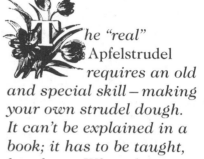

The "real" Apfelstrudel requires an old and special skill—making your own strudel dough. It can't be explained in a book; it has to be taught, hands-on. When done right, it is silky smooth, tissue-thin, and so elastic you can stretch it to cover your entire table. When done wrong, it's lumpy, full of holes, and so unwieldy you end up rolling it into a ball and using it as a weapon against whoever happens to stroll into your kitchen. So use phyllo dough and relax. Not as authentic but just as delicious.

Strudel does not keep well and is best enjoyed the same day it's baked. It will still taste good the next day, but the pastry will be limp and a bit soggy.

Using a third of the apples, spread them out evenly on the pastry, leaving a 1-inch margin at sides and 2 inches at top. Scatter a third of the bread crumbs, raisins, and walnuts on apples. Lifting the side of the towel nearest you, roll pastry up like a jelly roll. Using some butter to prevent sticking, fold up the sides or tuck under. Carefully lift strudel onto a buttered cookie sheet, seam side down. Brush all over with butter.

Repeat 2 more times until you have 3 strudels. Place them about 2 inches apart on cookie sheet. Bake for 20 to 25 minutes until golden brown. While still hot, heavily dust with powdered sugar. Let cool but don't chill.

To serve, carefully cut each strudel into 4 pieces. Pipe (with a pastry bag) or spoon a dollop of whipped cream on side or top and watch the strudel disappear!

Serves 12

Steven's Pumpkin Cheesecake

Crust

8 ounces (1½ cups) cinnamon-flavored graham
    cracker crumbs
½ cup butter, melted

Filling

3 8-oz. packages cream cheese, softened to room
    temperature
1¼ cups sugar
5 eggs
2 cups pumpkin purée (canned or frozen, but
    fresh is best*)
3 tablespoons rum
2 teaspoons vanilla
1 teaspoon ground cinnamon
½ teaspoon freshly grated ginger
¼ teaspoon freshly grated nutmeg
⅛ teaspoon *each* ground cloves, cardamom,
    and allspice

*To make fresh pumpkin purée, cut the pumpkin in
half and scrape out the seeds and fibrous material in
the center. Place the halves, cut side down, on a
greased baking sheet and bake in a 350° oven for 45
minutes or until tender. Scoop the pulp from the skin
and purée in a food processor. Fresh pumpkin purée
can be stored in the freezer for up to 2 months.*

Topping

2 cups sour cream
⅓ cup sugar
3 tablespoons rum

Mix the melted butter with the cracker crumbs
and press into the bottom and along the sides of
a 10-inch springform pan. Chill for 30 minutes.

*Every special fall
version of
the regular
cheesecake, perfect for the
holidays! "This dish,"
Steven writes, "was an
experiment in cooking
class one day, and it
promptly became my
favorite way to eat
cheesecake" (from A
Celebration of the Seasons,
a must-have cookbook by
Steven Raichlen).*

$\mathcal{P}$reheat oven to 325°.

$\mathcal{M}$eanwhile, beat the cream cheese and sugar together until smooth. Beat in the eggs, 1 at a time, until mixture is light and fluffy. Combine the pumpkin purée with the rum, vanilla and spices and beat until smooth. Beat the pumpkin mixture into the cream cheese mixture. Pour the filling into the crust and bake for 1 hour and 15 minutes or until set.

$\mathcal{F}$or topping, whisk the sour cream, sugar, and rum together until light and smooth. Spoon this mixture on top of the hot cheesecake. Turn off the oven and let the cake cool in the oven (this prevents the top from cracking). Then chill the pumpkin cheesecake for at least 6 hours (and up to 48 hours) before serving.

$\mathcal{S}$erves 10 to 12

Charlene's Cheese Cake

Crust
16 double graham crackers, crushed
1½ tablespoons sugar
4 tablespoons butter, melted
½ cup finely chopped walnuts

Filling
3 8-ounce packages cream cheese, softened to
   room temperature
5 eggs
1 cup sugar
1½ teaspoons vanilla

Topping
1½ pints sour cream
½ cup sugar
1½ teaspoons vanilla

Sauce (optional)
1 package frozen strawberries or raspberries

Frank grew up in New York, and to him, there was no cheesecake unless it was baked in "The City." Until we came to the inn. Until he tasted, for the first time, Charlene's version. As far as cheesecake is concerned, New York is now off the map. And we don't care where she got the recipe. All we know is that Charlene makes the best cheesecake in the whole wide world. We think you'll really love it.

Mix the cracker crumbs, sugar, butter, and nuts until well blended. Press into the bottom of a 10-inch springform pan. Set aside.

Preheat oven to 300°. For the filling, beat the cream cheese until smooth. Keep beating while adding the eggs, 1 at a time. Add sugar and vanilla and mix well. Pour onto the crust and bake for 1 hour. Remove from oven but don't turn off the heat. Allow the cake to cool for 5 minutes.

Blend sour cream, sugar, and vanilla for topping. Pour this mixture on top of the cake, return to oven, and bake 5 minutes more. Remove the cake and cool, then refrigerate until well chilled.

Purée the thawed berries in the food processor (you can add a bit of fresh lemon juice, a dash of orange liqueur, or sugar for added flavor). Pour a bit of the sauce in a band across each wedge of cake and serve. Pure heaven.

Serves 12 to 16

Husarenkrapferl
(Hussar's Cookies)

2⅓ cups flour
1 scant cup sugar
½ cup blanched and finely ground almonds
6 ounces unsalted butter, chilled
2 egg yolks
1 whole egg, slightly beaten with 1 tablespoon
   water
Apricot and/or red currant jelly

On a flat surface, mix flour, sugar, and almonds.
Cut the butter into this mixture and work into a
coarse, crumbly consistency. Add yolks and
quickly knead into a smooth ball, adding 1 to 2
tablespoons ice water if needed. Wrap and chill
for at least 30 minutes.

Preheat oven to 350°. Divide dough into
quarters and, using the palms of your hands, roll
each quarter into a smooth rope, about ½ inch
in diameter. Cut this rope into ½-inch pieces
and shape each piece into a little ball.
Place these balls, about 2 inches
apart, on an ungreased cookie
sheet. Indent each ball deeply,
using your finger or the flowered
tip of a whisk handle. You have
now shaped a "Krapferl."

Brush the cookies with the egg wash
and bake on top rack to a golden
color, about 15 to 20 minutes.
Fill the still-hot cookie centers
with a bit of either apricot or
currant jelly.

Makes about 50 cookies

A "Krapferl"
(meaning
"tiny donut"
in Austrian dialect) no
doubt commemorates
those dashing Hungarian
cavalry men, the hussars.
These cookies are
nicknamed "je laenger,
je besser" — the longer
they're stored, the better
they get. No need to freeze
them; just store in an
airtight container. They
keep and improve for
several weeks.

Vanillekipferl
(Vanilla Crescents)

2 cups flour
¼ cup plus 1 tablespoon sugar
1¾ cups blanched and finely ground almonds
7 ounces unsalted butter, chilled
1½ cups vanilla sugar [buy in specialty shops or make your own; if you make your own (recipe follows), do so at least a week in advance]

Another traditional Austrian favorite, to be served with tea, coffee, or anytime, but especially around Christmas.

On a flat surface, mix flour, sugar, and almonds. Work in the butter with your fingers or a pastry blender. Quickly knead ingredients together and form a smooth ball. Wrap and refrigerate for at least 1 hour.

Preheat oven to 350°. Place one-quarter of the dough on pastry board (keeping the rest chilled) and form a ¾-inch rope with your palms. Cut into teaspoon-size pieces. Mold each piece into a crescent, fat at the center and tapered on both ends. Carefully place on ungreased cookie sheet and bake for 15 to 20 minutes or until lightly colored.

Dip slightly cooled crescents in the vanilla sugar. Turn once to coat on both sides. Remove, let cool completely, then store in airtight container. They keep for many weeks.

Vanilla Sugar

4 cups granulated or powdered sugar
2 vanilla beans

Place sugar in a jar, stick vanilla beans all the way into the sugar, cover tightly, and store at room temperature. Shake once a day. After a week, sugar will have absorbed the vanilla flavor.

Makes about 50 cookies

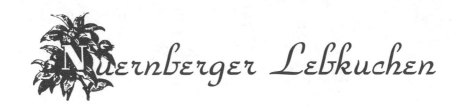

Nuernberger Lebkuchen

1 cup honey
¾ cup dark brown sugar
1 large egg, lightly beaten
2 tablespoons lemon juice
Grated peel from 1 lemon
2⅔ cups flour
1 teaspoon ground cinnamon
½ teaspoon *each* ground allspice, cloves, and
    nutmeg
½ teaspoon *each* salt and baking soda
⅓ cup minced candied citron
⅓ cup blanched and finely ground almonds
¾ pound almonds, peeled and halved

In Germany and Austria, Christmas baking traditionally begins in November with the preparation of Lebkuchen — spicy honey cookies that taste best if allowed to age for several weeks.

Heat honey over medium heat just until it begins to bubble. Cool slightly, then whisk in sugar, egg, lemon juice, and peel. Stir until smooth. Let cool to lukewarm.

In a large bowl, stir together flour, spices, salt, and baking soda. Add honey mixture, citron, and almonds. Stir until well blended; dough will be soft. Cover tightly with plastic wrap and refrigerate for at least 8 hours or for up to 2 days.

Preheat oven to 375°. Remove a quarter of the dough (keep the rest refrigerated). On a heavily floured board, roll out dough with a floured rolling pin to a thickness of ⅜ inch. Cut out desired shapes and place cookies 2 inches apart on baking sheet lined with lightly greased parchment paper. We usually use a large, 2-inch heart-shaped cookie cutter, but any simple shape will do. Or you can roll out a sheet of dough and cut it into rectangles about 1 x 2 inches. Bake 12 to 15 minutes or until golden brown.

Rum Glaze

1 cup powdered sugar
About 5 tablespoons rum

Whisk together until very smooth. Brush the still-hot cookies with the glaze. When cookies are completely cool and dry, pack into airtight containers and store at room temperature at least 2 weeks (will keep up to 3 months).

Makes about 40 large cookies

Walnut Kisses

Cookies

3 whole eggs
3 cups sugar
½ teaspoon baking powder
1 teaspoon vanilla
1 teaspoon ground cinnamon
Dash of ground cloves
Grated peel and juice of one-half lemon
2¼ ounces slivered almonds
4 cups walnuts, or 3 cups walnuts and 1 cup
   minced citron (optional)
1 small bag of walnut halves for garnish

Another recipe from Omi, my mother, who delighted our family with these cookies every Christmas. If she wasn't here for Christmas, she'd bake them in Austria and mail them. She didn't use airmail, but they survived the long journey remarkably well.

Blend eggs and sugar and beat until light and fluffy. Gradually add baking powder, vanilla, cinnamon, cloves, lemon peel, and juice. Grind the almonds in the food processor until they look like coarse bread crumbs. Add them to the batter. Repeat with the walnuts and add them to the batter, too. Mix well.

Preheat oven to 375 to 400°. Line a cookie sheet with lightly greased parchment paper. For each cookie, drop 1 teaspoon of the batter on the paper. Cookies will spread, so leave at least a 1-inch space between them. Put half a walnut on each cookie and bake them 20 minutes. Cookies should still be semisoft. Cool slightly and brush with rum glaze. Let dry completely and enjoy!

Rum Glaze

½ cup powdered sugar
2 tablespoons rum

Stir rum into sugar. Add a little water if necessary to get a smooth and creamy consistency. Brush over cookies.

Makes about 120 cookies

"Welcome to Snowvillage Inn" Cookies
(The Best Chocolate Chip Cookie You Ever Had)

1 pound butter, softened to room temperature
1 cup sugar
1 pound dark brown sugar
3 eggs
2 tablespoons vanilla
6 cups flour
1 tablespoon baking powder
1 tablespoon salt
4 cups real chocolate chips

As all our guests know, there's always a small gingham-lined basket stuffed with these delicious cookies awaiting them in their room — our way of saying "Hi, so glad you're here." And most of our guests have been so enthusiastic about this little treat that sometimes we wonder if that's why they keep coming back!

Place the butter in a large bowl and stir until fluffy. Using an electric hand mixer, beat in the sugars, eggs, and vanilla.

Mix the baking powder and salt into the flour. Gradually stir the flour into the cookie batter. Finally, add the chocolate chips. Batter will be quite stiff; you may have to finish the mixing with your hands on a pastry board, as if you were kneading bread.

Preheat oven to 350°. Drop a heaped tablespoon (we use the smallest ice cream scoop) of dough onto an ungreased cookie sheet and bake for about 9 minutes. Cookies will still be soft but become firm while cooling. If 9 minutes does not bake them right, turn up the oven to 375°. Let cookies cool completely before removing from baking sheet.

Note: These cookies freeze beautifully, so you can make a big batch and always have them on hand. Or you can divide this recipe in half (using 1 egg). In that case, you could use a stationary mixer with a dough hook for the final mixing — a lot easier!

Makes about 100 cookies

Naleshniki

(Crêpes with Farmer's Cheese and Maple Syrup)

The Crepes

1 cup flour
1 tablespoon sugar
Dash of salt
1 cup milk
⅓ cup water
3 eggs
4 tablespoons butter, melted
3 tablespoons butter for frying

Blend the flour, sugar, and salt. In another bowl, whisk the milk, water, eggs, and melted butter. Add the flour mixture and whisk until smooth (you can also use the food processor).

Heat a heavy 6- or 7-inch skillet or crêpe pan. Add a small amount of the frying butter to coat the pan. Drop about 3 tablespoons of the batter into the pan and at once tilt the pan to help spread the batter before it sets. Cook over medium heat for about 30 seconds on one side, flip over and finish with 15 seconds on the other. Repeat the process, adding butter as needed, until all the batter is used. Stack finished crêpes on a plate and keep warm.

The Filling

1 pound farmer's cheese (best in flavor, but cottage cheese works, too)
3 tablespoons sour cream
2 eggs
2 tablespoons sugar
½ teaspoon ground cinnamon
Zest and juice of ½ lemon

Funny how some things happen. At the grocery checkout line, a young woman behind me spotted my package of farmer's cheese. Suddenly lost in a state of ecstatic reverie, she described those blini-like little crepes with a funny name her Polish grandmother used to make. So of course I came home and told Rose.

Rose, or Rozalia, was born in Poland, you see. She has been at Snowvillage longer than we have and is our star waitress, top housekeeper, laundress, floral designer — in short, a true inn person. "Naleshniki," she nodded matter-of-factly. "I show you." And with that, she grabbed a skillet and ten minutes later we sampled these wonderful crêpe envelopes studded with light, lemony cheese. We added a New England touch by dousing them with maple syrup and decided right then and there that naleshniki were here to stay.

Mix all the ingredients in a bowl. Spread about 2 tablespoons on half of a crêpe. Flip the other half over the filling. Now fold that in half again so it looks like one-quarter of a crêpe. Repeat with all the crêpes. This can be done a day or two ahead of planned serving time. Cover and chill the crêpes. Bring to room temperature before frying.

To Finish

4 ounces butter
Maple syrup to taste

In a heavy skillet, melt a small amount of the butter. Add the stuffed crêpes and fry for 2 minutes on each side over medium heat. Serve with maple syrup.

Serve these crêpes for breakfast or with a fresh berry sauce for a great dessert.

Makes 12 to 14 crêpes, about 2 per person

Sachertorte

(A Traditional Viennese Chocolate Cake)

4½ ounces semisweet chocolate
9 tablespoons butter, room temperature
½ cup powdered sugar
6 eggs, separated
1 teaspoon vanilla
¼ teaspoon salt
½ cup granulated sugar
½ cup plus 1 tablespoon flour
1 cup apricot jam
1 tablespoon Curaçao liqueur
1 cup heavy cream, whipped

A true chocolate-lover's delight!

Preheat oven to 400°. Cover sides and bottom of a 10-inch springform pan with parchment paper.

Melt the chocolate in a double boiler and set aside. Whip the butter until light and fluffy. Beat in the powdered sugar, egg yolks, and vanilla. Add the melted chocolate and beat until well blended.

In a separate bowl, beat the egg whites, salt, and granulated sugar until very stiff. Gently fold this meringue into chocolate mixture, then fold in the flour.

$\mathcal{P}$our batter into the springform pan and bake for 20 minutes at 400 °. Reduce heat to 300° and bake 25 minutes longer. Let cake cool for 5 minutes, then remove from pan and place upside down on a flat surface. Remove springform and paper. When completely cooled, slice cake through the center horizontally into 2 even layers.

$\mathcal{H}$eat the apricot jam and stir in the Curaçao liqueur. Spread half the jam on the first layer, cover with the second layer, and spread the other half of the jam evenly over the top. Now make the glaze.

Glaze

9 ounces semisweet chocolate
1¼ cups sugar
½ cup plus 1 tablespoon cold water

$\mathcal{H}$eat these ingredients in a small pot over medium heat, stirring constantly, until chocolate has melted. Let simmer, stirring often, until candy thermometer reads 200°. Remove from heat, stir out the bubbles until glaze is smooth, then pour over top and sides of cake. Let cool and harden.

$\mathcal{S}$erve with a dollop of whipped cream alongside a narrow wedge of cake.

$\mathcal{S}$erves 16

Raspberry Torte

20 Ritz crackers (yes, really!)
1 cup finely chopped walnuts
1 teaspoon baking powder
3 egg whites, room temperature
1 cup sugar
1 teaspoon vanilla
¾ cup raspberry jelly
1 cup heavy cream
2 tablespoons shaved semisweet chocolate
8 fresh raspberries (optional)

An interesting combination of ingredients produces an outstanding dessert!

*P*reheat oven to 350° and thoroughly butter a 9-inch pie pan.

*C*rumble the crackers in a food processor (or place between waxed paper and crush with a rolling pin). Turn into a bowl and mix with the walnuts and baking powder. Set aside.

*B*eat the egg whites until fluffy. Keep beating while gradually adding the sugar and vanilla. Into the egg whites carefully *fold* (don't beat or the meringue will collapse) the crumb mixture. Turn into pie pan and bake for 30 minutes.

*W*hile still hot, spread pie with raspberry jelly. Top may crack and cave in a bit, but that's fine. Cool. Pie tastes best when done to this point one day ahead of time and chilled.

*J*ust before serving, whip the cream and spread over the raspberry jelly. Sprinkle with shaved chocolate and divide pie into 8 pieces. Garnish each piece with a fresh raspberry, if desired.

*S*erves 8

Index